Programming for Beginners

An Introduction to Learning Rust
Programming with Tutorials and
Hands-On Examples

Text Copyright © Lightbulb Publishing

All rights reserved. No part of this guide may be reproduced in any form without permission in writing from the publisher except in the case of brief quotations embodied in critical articles or reviews.

Legal & Disclaimer

The information contained in this book and its contents is not designed to replace or take the place of any form of medical or professional advice; and is not meant to replace the need for independent medical, financial, legal or other professional advice or services, as may be required. The content and information in this book has been provided for educational and entertainment purposes only.

The content and information contained in this book has been compiled from sources deemed reliable, and it is accurate to the best of the Author's knowledge, information, and belief. However, the Author cannot guarantee its accuracy and validity and cannot be held liable for any errors and/or omissions. Further, changes are periodically made to this book as and when needed. Where appropriate and/or necessary, you must consult a professional (including but not limited to your doctor, attorney, financial advisor or such other professional advisor) before using any of the suggested remedies, techniques, or information in this book.

Upon using the contents and information contained in this book, you agree to hold harmless the Author from and against any damages, costs, and expenses, including any legal fees potentially resulting from the application of any of the information provided by this book. This disclaimer applies to any loss, damages or injury caused by the use and application, whether directly or indirectly, of any advice or information presented, whether for breach of contract, tort, negligence, personal injury, criminal intent, or under any other cause of action.

You agree to accept all risks of using the information presented in this book.

You agree that by continuing to read this book, where appropriate and/or necessary, you shall consult a professional (including but not limited to your doctor, attorney, or financial advisor or such other advisor as needed) before using any of the suggested remedies, techniques, or information in this book.

Table of Contents

1. Introduction 1
2. Scope 3
3. Getting Started 5
   - 3.1 Install Rust on Windows 5
   - 3.2 Install Rust on Unix-like Operating Systems 8
   - 3.3 Compile and Execute Rust Programs 11
   - 3.4 Compile and Execute Demo 13
     - 3.4.1 Executing on Windows 13
     - 3.4.2 Executing on Unix-like OS 14
   - 3.5 cargo Tool 15
   - 3.6 Errors in Programs 18
4. Syntax 19
   - 4.1 Statements 19
   - 4.2 Comments 19
   - 4.3 Blocks 20
   - 4.4 Identifiers 21
   - 4.5 Keywords 21
   - 4.6 Basic Program Structure 22
   - 4.7 Crates, Modules and Path Separator (::) 23
5. Hello World! Rust Program 25
6. Basic Data Types 29
   - 6.1 Integer 29
   - 6.2 Floating Point 30

  6.3 Boolean 30

  6.4 Character 30

7. Variables and Constants 31

  7.1 Variables 31

    7.1.1 Variable Assignment 32

    7.1.2 String Variables 33

    7.1.3 Printing Variables 33

  7.2 Constants 35

8. Operators 39

  8.1 Arithmetic Operators 39

  8.2 Comparison Operators 43

  8.3 Logical Operators 45

  8.4 Bitwise Operators 46

  8.5 Compound Assignment Operators 48

9. Type Casting 51

10. User Input 55

  10.1 Reading Numbers 57

11. Decision Making 61

  11.1 if-else Construct 61

  11.2 match Construct 71

12. Loops 81

  12.1 while Loop 81

  12.2 loop Keyword 84

  12.3 for Loop 85

  12.4 Nested Loops 88

Table of Contents

1. Introduction 1
2. Scope 3
3. Getting Started 5
   3.1 Install Rust on Windows 5
   3.2 Install Rust on Unix-like Operating Systems 8
   3.3 Compile and Execute Rust Programs 11
   3.4 Compile and Execute Demo 13
      3.4.1 Executing on Windows 13
      3.4.2 Executing on Unix-like OS 14
   3.5 cargo Tool 15
   3.6 Errors in Programs 18
4. Syntax 19
   4.1 Statements 19
   4.2 Comments 19
   4.3 Blocks 20
   4.4 Identifiers 21
   4.5 Keywords 21
   4.6 Basic Program Structure 22
   4.7 Crates, Modules and Path Separator (::) 23
5. Hello World! Rust Program 25
6. Basic Data Types 29
   6.1 Integer 29
   6.2 Floating Point 30

    6.3 Boolean...30

    6.4 Character...30

7. Variables and Constants 31

    7.1 Variables...31

        7.1.1 Variable Assignment..32

        7.1.2 String Variables 33

        7.1.3 Printing Variables..33

    7.2 Constants 35

8. Operators..39

    8.1 Arithmetic Operators 39

    8.2 Comparison Operators 43

    8.3 Logical Operators 45

    8.4 Bitwise Operators 46

    8.5 Compound Assignment Operators......................................48

9. Type Casting 51

10. User Input 55

    10.1 Reading Numbers 57

11. Decision Making 61

    11.1 if-else Construct...61

    11.2 match Construct..71

12. Loops 81

    12.1 while Loop...81

    12.2 loop Keyword...84

    12.3 for Loop 85

    12.4 Nested Loops 88

13. Arrays ... 91
13.1 Accessing Array Elements ... 94
13.2 Arrays and Loops ... 96
13.3 Array Slices ... 103
14. Vectors ... 107
15. Strings ... 113
15.1 Concatenation ... 116
15.2 Replace ... 118
15.3 String Tokenization ... 119
16. Functions ... 121
16.1 Function Definition ... 121
16.2 Function call ... 122
16.3 Functions with parameters/arguments ... 124
16.4 Return value ... 126
16.5 Passing arrays and vectors to functions ... 129
16.6 Returning a vector from a function ... 131
16.7 Functions calling each other ... 133
17. Structures ... 135
18. Command Line Arguments ... 145
18.1 Fetching command line arguments ... 146
18.2 Numbers as command line arguments ... 147
19. Programming Examples ... 151
19.1 Fibonacci Series ... 151
19.2 Sum of digits of an integer ... 152
19.3 Reverse a number ... 153

19.4 Greatest number from command line arguments 154

19.5 Bubble Sort Algorithm.. 155

19.6 Array Reversal 157

19.7 Least Common Multiple (LCM)... 159

19.8 Greatest Common Divisor (GCD) 160

19.9 Prime or Composite 162

20. Final Words 165

1. Introduction

Rust is a computer programming language used to build *native applications* for various platforms. Native applications contain executable code which is native to a particular platform. Languages like C/C++ do very well when it comes to native application development but extra care needs to be taken to make those applications *memory safe*; whereas, applications built using Rust guarantee memory safety. An application is deemed memory safe when it is free from security vulnerabilities relating to memory access such as buffer overflows. Applications developed in Rust also have a performance advantage because they are native to specific platforms. A programming language like Python offers tons of functionalities and there are hundreds of frameworks for different areas such as image processing, data analytics, machine learning, etc. but the problem with such a language is that, it is an interpreted language. A Python interpreter is in charge of executing Python scripts line by line. Such a process will always be slower as compared to how a native application executes. No disrespect to Python, it is a great programming language, I am a Python developer myself (and a fan too!); the point I am trying to make here is – if performance is what you are looking for, you should go for a programming language which can build native applications.

Programming languages are classified using programming paradigms. Rust programming language supports multiple programming paradigms – *functional, generic, imperative, structured* and *concurrent*.

In the year 2006, a **Mozilla** employee named **Graydon Hoare** started developing Rust programming language as a personal project. In fact, some parts of **Mozilla Firefox** browser are written in Rust. Further, Mozilla sponsored the project in 2009 and was made public in 2010. Early Rust compiler was written in a language called **OCaml**. In the year 2011 a self hosting **LLVM** based compiler called **rustc** was released. As of 2021, Rust compilers are available for Windows, Linux, macOS and FreeBSD. These compilers can target applications for multiple platforms – Windows, Linux(x86 and ARM), macOS, FreeBSD, Web Assembly and Embedded Systems. It is also possible to build libraries for Android and iOS using Rust.

2. Scope

Rust is a multi-paradigm programming language aimed at developing native applications for specific target platforms. You can build almost anything with Rust – desktop applications, libraries for mobile applications, GUI applications (with appropriate bindings such as Qt), web applications, web services (eg. REST API), applications for embedded systems, IoT systems and much more. You can even build native applications for Raspberry Pi and other single board computers (SBC) using cross-compilation. Apart from some components of **Mozilla Firefox** browser written in Rust, there are many more successful projects built partially or fully using Rust. Some of them are – **Redox** (Unix-like OS), **Dropbox** (cloud storage service written in Python, Go, CoffeeScript and Rust), **OpenDNS**, **Stratis**, **Google Fuchsia**, some components of **Microsoft Azure IoT Edge** and many more!

What makes Rust popular is that it is an easy to learn language, syntactically quiet similar to C/C++. There is a huge collection of modules for accomplishing different objectives. For example, there are built-in modules to access databases such as MySQL, PostgreSQL, SQLite, etc. Keeping up with the latest trends, there are modules to even build blockchain applications! Apart from the built in modules, there are many open source frameworks for developing web applications, blockchain applications, building servers, etc. Some of the most used Rust frameworks are – **Rocket** (Used for building full-stack web applications), **Conrod** (2D GUI library), **Actix** (rendered HTTP web server), etc.

Who is this Book for?

This book is for anyone who is interested in learning Rust programming language.

What will I learn from this Book?

You will be learning the basic concepts of Rust. How to install Rust, get started with Rust programming and build console applications using various programming concepts.

Any pre-requisites?

A PC/Laptop with decently capable hardware is needed to install Rust and thereby write programs. No prior programming knowledge is needed to learn Rust. However, you should be very comfortable in using your system; especially, you should be comfortable with using the Command Prompt, Shell, Terminal, etc.

3. Getting Started

Rust programs are plaintext files. So, any text editor such as Notepad, WordPad, Notepad++, vi, emacs, etc. would suffice to write Rust programs. Rust compiler is needed build Rust applications. A compiler is a special kind of computer software that converts a program file into an executable application. Rust compiler is a part of *rustup* tool. Let us see how to install it and get the Rust environment to work.

3.1 Install Rust on Windows

Rust compiler for Windows depends on *Microsoft's MSVC* compiler, it is a part of *Microsoft C++ Build Tools* package. Log on to https://visualstudio.microsoft.com/visual-cpp-build-tools/, download Microsoft C++ Build Tools installer and install the tools. This process is quiet straight forward. Once Build Tools are installed, visit https://www.rust-lang.org/tools/install and download the Rust installer.

Note: You will need administrator rights in order to install Microsoft C++ Build Tools and Rust compiler.

Execute the Rust installer and you will be greeted with something like this:

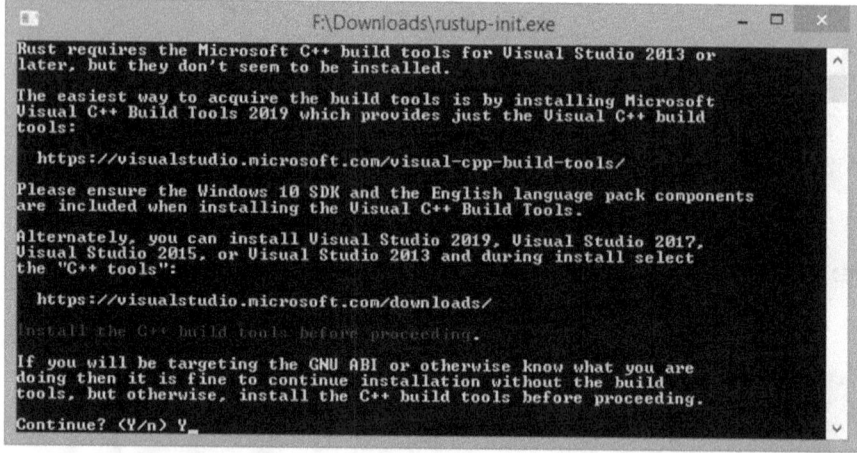

Type Y and hit Enter to continue.

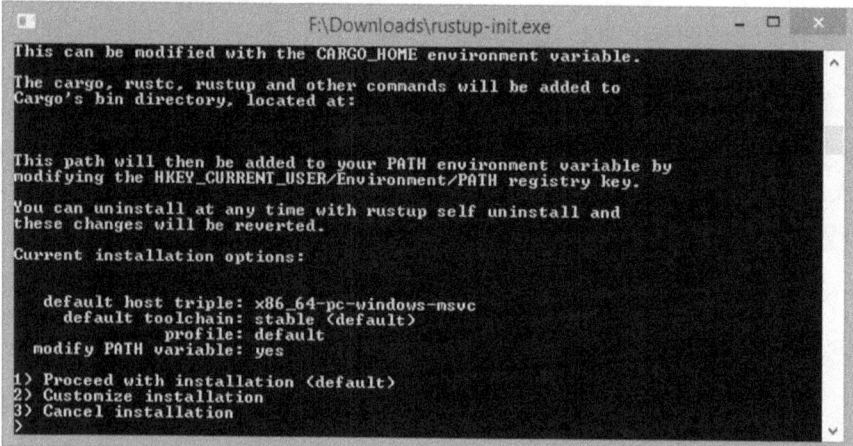

Here, you will be given options to customize the installation. Enter 1 to proceed with the default configuration.

3. Getting Started

```
F:\Downloads\rustup-init.exe

   default host triple: x86_64-pc-windows-msvc
     default toolchain: stable
                profile: default
  modify PATH variable: yes

1) Proceed with installation (default)
2) Customize installation
3) Cancel installation
>1

info: profile set to 'default'
info: setting default host triple to x86_64-pc-windows-msvc
info: syncing channel updates for 'stable-x86_64-pc-windows-msvc'
info: latest update on 2020-12-31, rust version 1.49.0 (e1884a8e3 2020-12-29)
info: downloading component 'cargo'
  3.4 MiB /   3.4 MiB (100 %) 997.3 KiB/s in  4s ETA:  0s
info: downloading component 'clippy'
  1.6 MiB /   1.6 MiB (100 %) 615.5 KiB/s in  2s ETA:  0s
info: downloading component 'rust-docs'
 13.8 MiB /  13.8 MiB (100 %)   1.0 MiB/s in 14s ETA:  0s
info: downloading component 'rust-std'
 18.9 MiB /  18.9 MiB (100 %) 1014.4 KiB/s in 22s ETA:  0s
info: downloading component 'rustc'
  9.0 MiB /  42.9 MiB ( 21 %) 803.2 KiB/s in 10s ETA: 43s
```

The installation process will now begin. Several files will have to be downloaded so this process may take a few minutes to complete.

Once the installation is done, you should see something like this:

```
F:\Downloads\rustup-init.exe

info: using up to 500.0 MiB of RAM to unpack components
info: installing component 'clippy'
info: installing component 'rust-docs'
 13.8 MiB /  13.8 MiB (100 %) 348.8 KiB/s in 1m 13s ETA:  0s
info: installing component 'rust-std'
 18.9 MiB /  18.9 MiB (100 %)   2.4 MiB/s in  8s ETA:  0s
  4 IO-ops /   4 IO-ops (100 %)   1 IOPS in  2s ETA:  0s
info: installing component 'rustc'
 42.9 MiB /  42.9 MiB (100 %)   5.1 MiB/s in 11s ETA:  0s
  9 IO-ops /   9 IO-ops (100 %)   8 IOPS in  1s ETA:  0s
info: installing component 'rustfmt'
  2.0 MiB /   2.0 MiB (100 %)   2.0 MiB/s in  1s ETA:  0s
info: default toolchain set to 'stable-x86_64-pc-windows-msvc'

  stable-x86_64-pc-windows-msvc installed - rustc 1.49.0 (e1884a8e3 2020-12-29)

Rust is installed now. Great!

To get started you need Cargo's bin directory (%USERPROFILE%\.cargo\bin) in
your PATH environment variable. Future applications will automatically
have the correct environment, but you may need to restart your current shell.

Press the Enter key to continue.
```

In order to check if the Rust compiler is installed successfully, open the command prompt and enter the following command:

cargo --version

If you see something like this, it means that Rust environment has been successfully set up and you can now use it to build Rust programs.

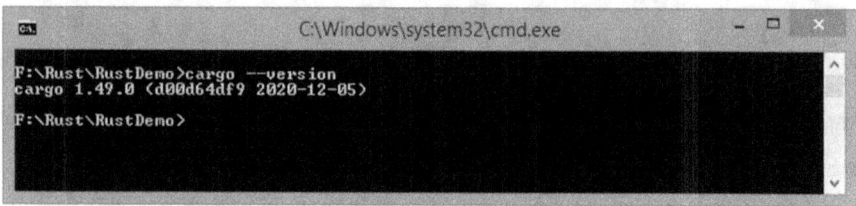

If you see something like this – *'cargo' is not recognized as an internal or external command, operable program or batch file.* It either means there is a problem with the installation or the *PATH* variable has not been set correctly. In such a case, check the environment *PATH* variable using the *echo %PATH%* command, if *bin* directory of Rust has not been added to it, add it manually through *System Properties* (*Windows Key + Pause Break*). If the *PATH* variable is correctly set and *cargo* command can still not be found, then go through the installation process once again.

3.2 Install Rust on Unix-like Operating Systems

Rust compiler on Unix-like operating systems depends on the *GCC compiler toolchain*. If you do not have it installed on your system, install it before proceeding. Installing Rust on Unix-like operating systems like Linux, macOS, FreeBSD, etc. is slightly different than installing it on Windows. Open Shell/Terminal, enter the following command and press Enter:

curl --proto '=https' --tlsv1.2 -sSf https://sh.rustup.rs | sh

3. Getting Started

This command will download *rustup-ini.sh* shell script. This shell script will then download the correct version of *rustup* for your system. This process is automatic. Here is what you should see:

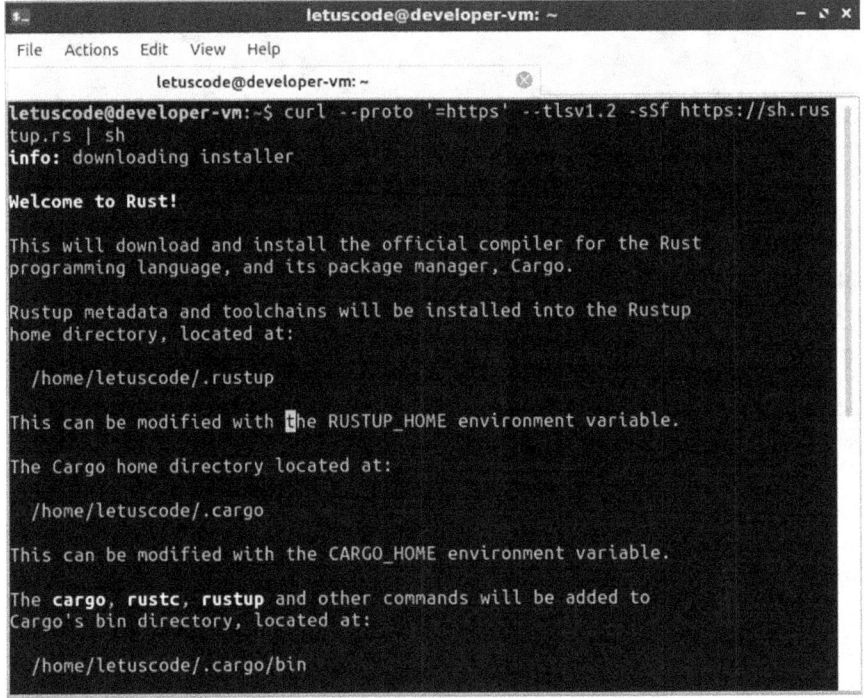

Read and understand the instructions carefully.

Scroll down to the bottom, type 1 and hit Enter:

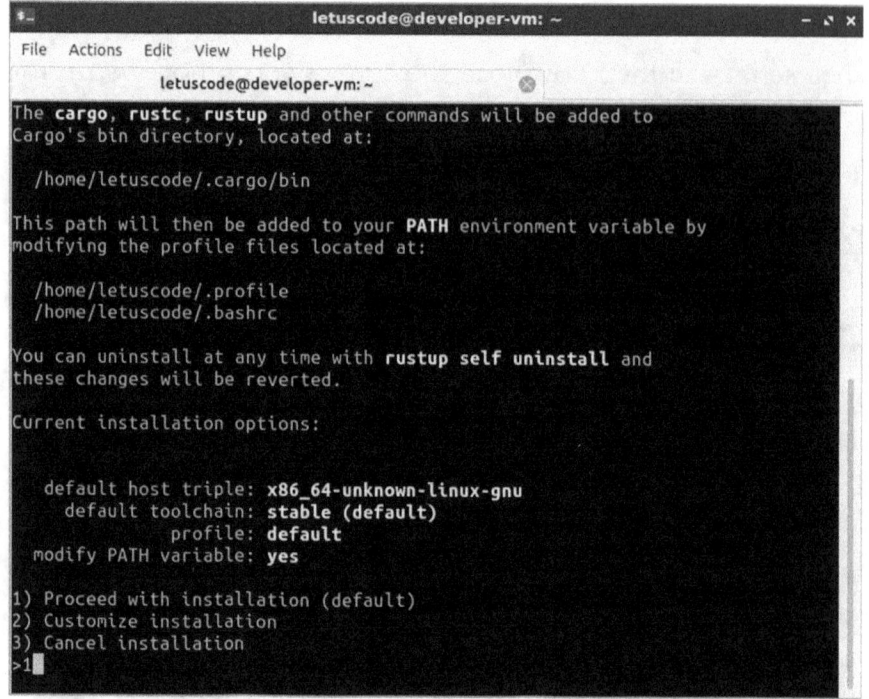

The installation process will now begin. Once the installation finishes, important files such as cargo, rustup, rustc, etc. will be located at:

/*home*/*<user>*/*.cargo*/*bin*

The above directory should be added to the **PATH** environment variable. This variable can be modified inside the profile files:

/*home*/*<user>*/*.bashrc*

/*home*/*<user>*/*.profile*

Note: Adding /*home*/*<user>*/*.cargo*/*bin* to the **PATH** variable makes it possible to access the Rust compiler from anywhere.

This step is very important. Once this is done, restart the Shell/Terminal.

In order to check if Rust has been installed correctly on your system, open the Terminal/Shell and enter the following command:

cargo --version

You should see something like this:

3.3 Compile and Execute Rust Programs

A Rust program is a simple plaintext file having the extension *.rs*. A program file is also known as source code, code, source file or simply source. This file has instructions that specify what the target application should do. Rust compiler turns a Rust program into an executable application. Here is a conceptual diagram of this process:

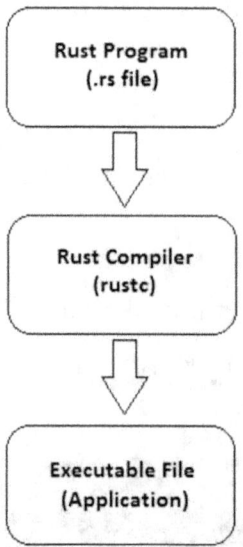

Of course, there is more to compilation procedure than just three blocks but the above diagram is accurate – simplicity is chosen for the sake of understanding.

Regardless of the operating system, Rust compiler can be invoked using the **rustc** command. Majority of the times, you will be using this command to build an executable application from a Rust source file as follows:

rustc <Rust Source File>

Example:

rustc myprog.rs

In the above command, we supply *<Rust Source File>* as a command line argument to **rustc**. If the compilation is successful, the above command will build an executable file. That file needs to be executed in order to run the application.

3.4 Compile and Execute Demo

Let us see compilation and execution procedure in action. Open your favourite text editor, copy-paste the following code, save it as *TestRust.rs*:

```
fn main() {
 println!("Hello from Rust!");
}
```

Open *Command Prompt/Shell/Terminal*, navigate to the directory where TestRust.rs is present and enter the following command:

rustc TestRust.rs

If the compilation is successful, the executable binary will be generated. Let us see how to deal with it on different operating systems:

3.4.1 Executing on Windows

On Windows, if the compilation of a Rust program is successful, an executable file with *.exe* extension will be generated. For example, if the source file's name is *TestRust.rs*, upon its successful compilation, *TestRust.exe* will be generated. In order to run the executable file in the command prompt, simply type in the full file name:

<Executable File Name>.exe

Example:

TestRust.exe

Here is a recap of the compilation and execution process – compile a Rust program using *rustc <Program File>.rs* and execute it as *<Program File>.exe*. The following commands are used to compile and execute *TestRust.rs*:

rustc TestRust.rs

TestRust.exe

Here is what you will see if you followed the exact procedure:

```
P:\Rust>rustc TestRust.rs
P:\Rust>TestRust.exe
Hello from Rust!
P:\Rust>
```

3.4.2 Executing on Unix-like OS

Upon successful compilation of a Rust program on Unix-like OS, an executable binary will be generated. Executable files on Linux and other Unix-like operating systems do not carry any extension. For example, if you successfully compile a Rust file called *HelloLinux.rs*, an executable file called *HelloLinux* will be generated. An executable file can be run as *./<Executable File>*. In case of *HelloLinux*, it can be executed as *./HelloLinux*. Let us go back to the *TestRust.rs* example. You would compile the file as:

rustc TestRust.rs

If the compilation is successful, an executable file called *TestRust* will be generated. This file can be executed as

./TestRust

You should see something like this when you compile and execute:

Note: The *dir* command shown in the above screenshot is not mandatory for compilation and execution. Its only purpose was to show the presence of *TestRust* executable file post compilation.

3.5 cargo Tool

The Rust environment comes with a very useful tool called *cargo*. This tool is used to build large Rust projects with multiple source files. In most of the programming examples in this book, we will be using only *rustc*. The purpose of this section is to demonstrate the utility of cargo. The usage of cargo remains the same across operating systems. Using cargo, a new project is created first, then it is built and upon successful compilation, it is run. Let us go through this process one step at a time.

Step 1 – Create Project

A new project can be created using cargo as follows:

cargo new <project_name>

Example:

cargo new my_project

The above command will create a new directory called *my_project*. Inside it, a file called *Cargo.toml* will be created. This is like a manifest file carrying metadata about the project. This file is of no significance to us as of now. A directory called *src* will be created and inside that a Rust source file called *main.rs* will be created. This file will have a standard *"Hello, world!"* template program. You need to make changes to this file if you plan to build applications using cargo instead of *rustc*. Let us create a project called *demo_rust:*

- Get inside this directory using *cd* command

- Display the contents using *ls* command

- Get inside the *src* directory using *cd* command again

- Display the contents of *src* directory using *ls* command

- Print the contents of *main.rs* file using cat command

```
letuscode@developer-vm:~/Rust$ cargo new demo_rust
    Created binary (application) `demo_rust` package
letuscode@developer-vm:~/Rust$ cd demo_rust/
letuscode@developer-vm:~/Rust/demo_rust$ ls
Cargo.toml  src
letuscode@developer-vm:~/Rust/demo_rust$ cd src/
letuscode@developer-vm:~/Rust/demo_rust/src$ ls
main.rs
letuscode@developer-vm:~/Rust/demo_rust/src$ cat main.rs
fn main() {
    println!("Hello, world!");
}
letuscode@developer-vm:~/Rust/demo_rust/src$
```

Step 2 – Build Project

The next step is to build the project. Open ***Command Prompt/Shell/Terminal***, navigate to the directory of the Rust project you want to build – ***demo_rust*** in this case and enter the following command:

cargo build

This command will implicitly fire up the ***rustc*** command. If there are multiple compilable source files, all of them will be compiled. If there are no problems with your source files and the build is therefore successful, the executable file will be placed inside ***<project_name>/target/debug/*** directory.

Step 3 – Run Project

In order to run a project, use the following command:

cargo run

The above command will execute the default target executable located inside ***<project_name>/target/debug/*** directory.

In case of ***demo_rust***, here is how ***cargo build*** and ***cargo run*** would look like:

```
letuscode@developer-vm:~/Rust$ cd demo_rust/
letuscode@developer-vm:~/Rust/demo_rust$ cargo build
   Compiling demo_rust v0.1.0 (/home/letuscode/Rust/demo_rust)
    Finished dev [unoptimized + debuginfo] target(s) in 52.93s
letuscode@developer-vm:~/Rust/demo_rust$ cargo run
    Finished dev [unoptimized + debuginfo] target(s) in 0.14s
     Running `target/debug/demo_rust`
Hello, world!
letuscode@developer-vm:~/Rust/demo_rust$
```

Alternatively, after successfully building the project using cargo build command, you can manually run the executable file placed inside *<project_name>/target/debug/* directory as follows:

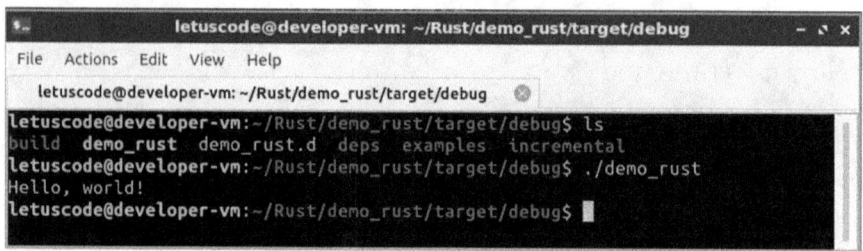

3.6 Errors in Programs

Errors can be broadly classified into two categories – *compile-time errors* and *runtime errors*. Compile time errors occur mostly because of the syntax. Errors resulting from wrong syntax are also known as *syntax errors.* If there are syntax errors in your program, the Rust compiler will pin point them most of the times. Yet, it is still a good idea to check a program thoroughly before compiling.

4. Syntax

This chapter onwards, we will be learning the actual programming concepts of Rust thereby be able to write our own programs. Rust is a case-sensitive programming language. We humans may treat the same words in different cases as the same but the Rust compiler will treat them differently. For example, words "Programming", "programming" and "PROGRAMMING" may look the same to us but each word will be treated differently by the compiler.

4.1 Statements

A statement carries out a meaningful computational task. These tasks can be anything such as adding numbers, printing something on the console, reading from a file, etc. Statements in Rust end with a semi-colon (;). It is best practice to have one statement on one line although it is possible to separate multiple statements using a semi-colon on a single line. This is a widely accepted coding practice and also encourages code readability. Some examples of statements are:

println!("Hi!");

let x = 30;

a = b * c;

4.2 Comments

Comments are completely ignored by the compiler and thus have no outcome on the output of the program. There are no hard and fast rules regarding when and how to use comments.

Developers use comments to mark or explain a piece of code; can also carry notes for other developers. Rust offers single-line and multi-line comments. Single line comments begin with **double-slash (//)** and must terminate on the same line. Multi line comments are like a block of comments and are enclosed within this character sequence – **slash-asterisk (/*)** and asterisk-slash *(*/)*; such comments can span across multiple lines.

Single Line Comments:

//This is a comment

//This is yet another single-line

Multi-Line Comment"

/*

Comments can span across multiple lines when you use this char sequence.

On each new line, nothing new needs to be done, simply type.

*/

Note: This book contains many programming examples. Wherever possible, parts of code have been explained using comments. Make sure that you read the comments to better understand a particular program.

4.3 Blocks

A block of code in Rust is a group of statements enclosed within curly brackets ({ }). Here is an example:

```
{
println!("Hello");
println!("This is a block!")
}
```

Blocks are used heavily in decision making, loops, functions, etc.

4.4 Identifiers

Identifiers are used to identify variables, functions, etc. Identifier names can contain alphanumeric characters and underscores; but has to start with either an underscore or an alphabet.

4.5 Keywords

Keywords in a programming language are reserved words which cannot be used as identifier names. Keywords have a specific meaning which tells the resultant application what to do. Here is a list of all keywords in Rust:

as	async	await
break	const	continue
crate	dyn	else
enum	extern	flase
fn	for	if
impl	in	let
loop	match	mod
move	mut	pub

ref	return	self
Self	static	struct
super	trait	true
type	union	unsafe
use	where	while

The keywords mentioned in the previous table are presently in use and here are the ones reserved for future use:

abstract	become	box
final	macro	override
try	typeof	unsize
do	priv	virtual
yield		

4.6 Basic Program Structure

Most of the programs that we will be writing in this book will be compiled as stand-alone console applications. For such a program, there should be a mandatory *main function* defined with the *fn* keyword. A main function serves as an entry point to a program. That is, a program will begin executing from the first statement of the main function. Here is the general syntax:

fn main () {

  //Statements here

}

Let us try to compile and execute the above program:

As seen, the program compiles successfully into an executable file. Further, we execute the executable file. We do not see anything on the console. That is because we literally have an empty main function. The execution enters and exits the main function without doing anything meaningful.

4.7 Crates, Modules and Path Separator (::)

A crate is like a library which can contain several modules. A module is a collection of several items such as functions, user defined data types, etc. The path separator (::) is used to pin point an item or module. For example, consider the following statement:

std::Vec::new()

std is the crate (Rust standard library), **Vec** is the module and **new()** is the item (a method in this case). Many of the concepts taught in this book make use of the path separator.

5. Hello World! Rust Program

We have learned the basic syntax of Rust and the basic program structure. Let us learn a few more things needed to print a message on the console – the infamous *Hello World!* Program. In Rust, there are many predefined macros and functions which can be used to carry out a certain tasks. We will learn more about such programming concepts throughout the book but for now, understand that a macro/function is a piece of code written to perform one or more computational tasks. In order to print something on the console, you can use one of these two macros – *print* and *println*. The *print* macro prints a formatted string on the same line while the *println* macro prints on a new line. The usage of both these macros are syntactically similar, both accept a formatted string which is then printed on the console. A string is a sequence of characters; for now, we will only learn to print a string and worry about a formatted string later.

Here is a general syntax of *print* and *println*:

print!(<String to be printed>)

println!(<String to be printed on a new line>)

Example:

print!("Hello World!")

println!("Hello World!")

Let us put all that we have learned so far and write a program to print *"Hello World!"* on the console. We know that a basic stand alone program needs a *main* function (declared with an *fn* keyword) to begin execution and *print* or *println* macro to print something on the console:

```rust
//Hello World! Program
//Main function
fn main () {
    //println! macro to print a message on the console
    println!("Hello World!")
}
```

Output:

Let us take a few more examples and try to print different things on the screen. The previous example used println macro, let us see how print works:

```rust
//Usage of print and println
//Main function
fn main () {
    //println! macro to print a message on new line
    println!("Hello");
    println!("World!");
    //println! macro to print a message on the same line
    print!("Hello");
    print!("World");
}
```

5. Hello World! Rust Program

Output:

```
F:\Rust>rustc printdemo.rs
F:\Rust>printdemo.exe
Hello
World!
HelloWorld
F:\Rust>
```

As seen, the print macro will write text on the same line even if you use a new print macro. You can use escape sequences \n and \t for newline and tab-space respectively. Here is an example:

```rust
fn main () {
    println!("This should be printed on the first
    line.\nAnd this on the next one!");
    print!("\nLeaving another line.\tThis is what a
    tab-space indent looks like.\nHappy
    Programming!\n");
}
```

Output:

```
F:\Rust>rustc escapeseq.rs
F:\Rust>escapeseq.exe
This should be printed on the first line.
And this on the next one!

Leaving another line.   This is what a tab-space indent looks like.
Happy Programming!
F:\Rust>
```

Note: Being able to print a constant string on the console is an essential concept to learn. Before moving on to the next chapters which deal with more advanced programming concepts, you should be very comfortable with being able to compile & execute Rust programs and print different messages on the console.

6. Basic Data Types

Data types are used to categorize different types of data. In the previous chapter we saw how to print a string on the console. String is one type of data; Similarly, numbers belong to another data type. Rust is a statically typed language. That is, it must know the data types of variables. In Rust, data types can be broadly classified in to two main categories – scalar types and compound types. We will look at scalar data types in this chapter. Compound types will be covered as and when we come across them.

Rust offers four scalar types – Integer, Floating point, Boolean and Character. Scalar types are used to represent a single value at a time.

6.1 Integer

Integers are used to represent numbers which do not have fractional component. Signed integers are used to represent positive as well as negative numbers while unsigned integers are used to represent zero or positive numbers. Here are the different types of integers supported by Rust:

Integer Size	Signed Integer	Unsigned Integer
8 bit	i8	u8
16 bit	i16	u16
32 bit	i32	u32
64 bit	i64	u64
128 bit	i128	u128
arch (Architecture Specific)	isize	usize

Note: When you use the arch type, the size of the integer will be set according to the platform. That is, on 32-bit machines, it will be 32-bit, on 64-bit machines it will be 64-bit and so on.

6.2 Floating Point

Floating point types are used to store numbers having fractional component. Rust offers 32-bit and 64-bit floats given by *f32* and *f64* respectively. When no specific type is specified, f64 is assumed to be the default float type.

Note: For integers and floats, you can use underscore as number separator. This increases code readability. For example, one million is generally written using commas like this – 1,000,000. In Rust, this can be written as 1_000_000. This is much better than writing simply 1000000.

6.3 Boolean

A Boolean data type (*bool*) can hold one of two values – *true* or *false*. There are various applications of these data types. Some of the prominent ones are decision making, loops, etc.

6.4 Character

A character data type (*char*) is used to store a single character value. Apart from ASCII characters, Rust also supports Unicode characters within the following rangers – *U+0000* to *U+D7FF* and *U+E000* to *U+10FFF*.

A character value needs to be enclosed within single quotes. For example – 'X', '$', '0', etc. When dealing with Unicode characters, the \u escape character sequence is used. For example – '\u{1F601}', '\u{1F602}', etc.

7. Variables and Constants

When we want to store data, it needs some memory space. That memory space has a unique address. A variable is a name given to a memory location. Memory locations are addressed using hexadecimal values most of the times. Being able to give it a name is very convenient as opposed to dealing directly with hexadecimal memory addresses. In fact, there are some programming languages such as assembly language which allow you to directly access memory locations using their addresses. Such languages are generally difficult to learn and hence not so popular these days.

7.1 Variables

Variables can be broadly classified into two types – **mutable variables** and **immutable variables**. A variable is said to be a mutable one if its value is allowed to be changed through the course of the program where as the value of an immutable variable cannot be changed once it is set. The *let* keyword is used to declare variables as follows:

//Immutable variables

let <variable> name:<Optional Data Type>;

//Mutable variables

let mut <variable name>:<Optional Data Type>;

Example:

let num:i32;

let x:f64;

let z;

let mut flag:bool;

let mut add;

Variables can also be initialized at the time of declaration as follows:

//Immutable variables

let <variable name>:<Optional Data Type> = <Initial Value>;

//Mutable variables

let mut <variable name>:<Optional Data Type> = <Initial Value>;

Example:

let name = "Zico";

let age:isize = 39;

let mut score:f64 = 8.95;

7.1.1 Variable Assignment

Values of variables can be assigned using the **equal to sign (=)**. The value on the right will be assigned to the variable on the left. Be advised – the value of an immutable variable if initialized, cannot be changed at a later point in the program; if not initialized, it can be set only once. A mutable variable's value can be changed as many times as desired.

Here are a few examples of variable assignment:

let x:u32;

let mut y:f64 = 7.5;

x = 60;

y = -7.8;

7.1.2 String Variables

Strings are of two types in Rust – ***String literals*** and ***Object type***. There is a whole chapter on strings in this book which talks about strings in more detail. For now, let us take a look at string literals. A string is a sequence of characters. A string literal is of the data type ***&str***. A simple string can be formed by enclosing the sequence of characters within double quotes. Here are a few examples of string variables:

let name:&str = "Jordan";

let address = "Phoenix";

let country:&str;

country = "USA";

7.1.3 Printing Variables

We have seen how to declare variables, how to initialize them and how to set their values. Let us now learn how to print their values on the console. We will use ***print*** And ***prinln*** macros to print values on the screen. In ***Chapter 5*** we learned that these macros can be used to print a string. Now, we will learn how to print a basic formatted string. Within the string, we can use the '***{}***' substitution token. This will be substituted by the corresponding argument. Consider the following code snippet:

let name:&str = "Lilly";

let age:isize = 32;

let country:&str = "UK";

println!("Name = {} Age = {} Country = {}", name, age, country);

First *{}* will be substituted by **name**, the second by **age** and the third by **country** as follows:

println!("Name = {} Age = {} Country = {}", name, age, country);

The output will look like:

Name = Lilly Age = 32 Country = UK

Let us now write a program where we will declare a few variables and print their values:

```
//Variables Demo
fn main () {
  //Declare and initialize some variables
  let name:&str = "Willow";
  let age:usize = 36;
  let gender:char = 'F';
  let married:bool;
  let country = "Australia";
  //Set the value of married boolean variable
  married = true;
  //Print everything
```

7. Variables and Constants

```
    println!("\nName: {}\tAge: {}\tGender: {}\nMarried: {}\tCountry: {}", name, age, gender, married, country);
}
```

Output:

```
F:\Rust>rustc vardemo.rs
F:\Rust>vardemo.exe
Name: Willow    Age: 36 Gender: F
Married: true   Country: Australia
F:\Rust>
```

7.2 Constants

A constant is an identifier whose value cannot be changed. In the previous section, we read a similar definition – *immutable variables*. Values of immutable variables cannot be changed and the same thing applies to constants. Well, in that case why do we need these two different programming concepts? Would any one of these not suffice? Technically, yes – as a beginner you could get away with using either one of these to get your job done. However, constants and immutable variables co-exist for many reasons. The explanation to how these two concepts differ technically is beyond the scope of this book. The short answer to this question is – constants are a compile-time representation. A constant is an alias given to a value. That is, a constant is substituted by its value at the time of compilation it self. Where as, in case of a variable (mutable or immutable) its value is fetched from the relevant memory location during run-time. Here is the general syntax to declare constants:

const <Constant Name>:<Data Type> = <Initial Value>

Example:

const PI:f64 = 3.14;

Let us take a programming example on constants:

```rust
//Constant Demo
fn main () {
    //Declare and initialize some constants
    const NAME:&str = "Yulia";
    const AGE:usize = 23;
    const GENDER:char = 'F';
    const MARRIED:bool = false;
    const COUNTRY:&str = "Russia";
    //Print everything
    println!("\nName: {}\tAge: {}\tGender: {}\nMarried: {}\tCountry: {}", NAME, AGE, GENDER, MARRIED, COUNTRY);
}
```

Output:

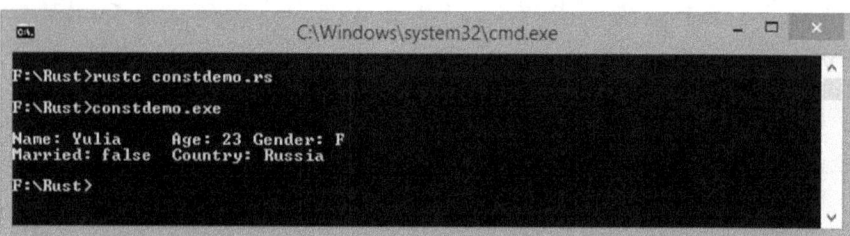

Note:

- Variables and constants follow the same naming rules. Can contain alphanumeric characters and underscore; but cannot start with a number.

7. Variables and Constants

- It is a good practice to use all upper case letters for naming constants. Even if you do not, your program will work perfectly fine but the compiler will give you a warning.

- Specifying the data type of a constant is mandatory at the time of declaration.

- Always use meaningful names for variables and constants. For example, if you want to store the age of a person, it makes sense to name the variable as age or person_age or anything relevant as compared to something random like n, x, etc.

8. Operators

An operator is a symbol or a sequence of symbols used to carry out a computational operation. An operation could be anything such as multiplying three numbers, checking if one variable is greater than the other, etc. Rust supports the following categories of operators – Arithmetic Operators, Comparison Operators, Logical Operators, Bitwise Operators and Compound Assignment Operators. Let us take a look at each categories of operators:

8.1 Arithmetic Operators

Arithmetic Operators are used to perform mathematical operations such as addition, subtraction, multiplication, etc. Here are all the supported arithmetic operators:

Operator	Description	Sample Usage	Explanation
+	Addition	x + y	Adds all operands, returns sum of the operands.
-	Subtraction	x - y	Subtracts operand on the right from the operand on the left and returns the difference.
*	Multiplication	x * y	Multiplies operands and returns the product.
/	Division	x / y	Performs division and returns the quotient.
%	Arithmetic Remainder	x % y	Performs division and returns the remainder. Operands needs to be of integer type.

Note:

- When you divide an integer by another integer, the quotient will be an integer even if mathematically the quotient is suppose to be a float, the fractional part will be discarded and only the integer part will be considered.

- When variables of different type are used in a mathematical expression, the variables need to be converted to the appropriate data types. We will learn more about this in the next chapter.

- The print and println macros can be used to directly print the result of an expression. Instead of specifying a variable as an argument, an expression can be specified. In such a case, the expression will be evaluated first and the resulting value will be printed.

Let us write a program to demonstrate the usage of arithmetic operators:

```
//Arithmetic Operators
fn main() {
    //Declare some variables
    let a:isize = 70;
    let b:isize = 30;
    let x:f64 = 5.8;
    let y:f64 = -3.2;
    let sum:isize;
    let diff:isize;
    let prod:f64;
    let modulus:isize;
    let quo:f64;
    //Perform arithmetic operations
    sum = a + b;
```

8. Operators

```
    diff = a - b;
    modulus = a % b;
    prod = x * y;
    quo = x / y;
    
    println!("\na = {} b = {} \n\nx = {} y = {}", a, b, x, y);
    println!("\na + b = {} \na - b = {} \na % b = {}", sum, diff, modulus);
    println!("\nx * y = {} x / y = {}", prod, quo);
}
```

Output:

```
F:\Rust>rustc arithmeticoperators.rs
F:\Rust>arithmeticoperators.exe
a = 70 b = 30
x = 5.8 y = -3.2
a + b = 100
a - b = 40
a % b = 10
x * y = -18.56 x / y = -1.8124999999999998
F:\Rust>
```

Let us write a program to demonstrate how mathematical expressions can be realized using multiple operators in a single statement. We will write the expressions for the basic formulas of algebra:

$(a + b)^2 = a^2 + 2ab + b^2$

$(a - b)^2 = a^2 - 2ab + b^2$

$a^2 - b^2 = (a + b)(a - b)$

$(a + b)^3 = a^3 + b^3 + 3ab(a + b)$

$(a - b)^3 = a^3 - b^3 - 3ab(a - b)$

When there are multiple terms in an expression, brackets can be used just like in mathematics. For example, $a^3 + b^3 + 3ab(a + b)$ can be written as $(a * a * a) + ((3 * a * b) * (a + b)) + (b * b * b)$. Here is the program:

```
//Algebra Formulas
fn main() {
    //Declare some variables
    let a:isize = 5;
    let b:isize = 8;
    let a_p_b_2:isize;
    let a_m_b_2:isize;
    let a_p_b_3:isize;
    let a_m_b_3:isize;
    let a_2_m_b_2:isize;
    //Algebra expressions
    a_p_b_2 = (a * a) + (2 * a * b) + (b * b);
    a_m_b_2 = (a * a) - (2 * a * b) + (b * b);
    a_2_m_b_2 = (a + b) * (a - b);
    a_p_b_3 = (a * a * a) + ((3 * a * b) * (a + b)) + (b * b * b);
    a_m_b_3 = (a * a * a) - ((3 * a * b) * (a - b)) - (b * b * b);
    //Print everything
    println!("\na = {} b = {}", a, b);
    println!("\n(a + b)^2 = {}", a_p_b_2);
    println!("\n(a - b)^2 = {}", a_m_b_2);
    println!("\na^2 - b^2 = {}", a_2_m_b_2);
    println!("\n(a + b)^3 = {}", a_p_b_3);
    println!("\n(a - b)^3 = {}", a_m_b_3);
}
```

Output:

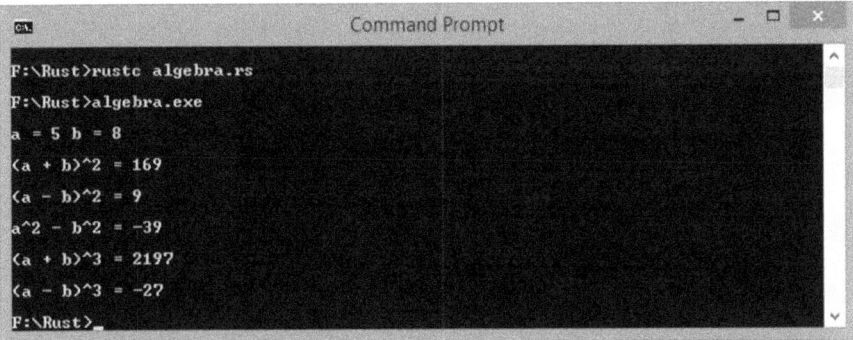

8.2 Comparison Operators

Comparison operators are used to compare two or more variables/values/constants. These are also known as *relational operators*.

Operator	Description	Sample Usage	Explanation
==	Equal To	x == y	Returns *true* if the values of the given operands are *EQUAL*, *false* otherwise.
!=	Not Equal To	x != y	Returns *true* if the values of the given operands are *NOT EQUAL*, *false* otherwise.
<	Less Than	x < y	Returns *true* if the value of the left operand is less than the value of the operand on the right, returns *false* otherwise.
>	Greater Than	x > y	Returns *true* if the value of the left operand is greater than the value of the operand on the right, returns *false* otherwise.
<=	Less Than OR Equal To	x <= y	Returns true if the value of the left operand is less than *OR EQUAL TO* the value of the operand on the right, *false* otherwise.
>=	Greater Than OR Equal To	x >= y	Returns *true* if the value of the left operand is greater than *OR EQUAL TO* the value of the operand on the right, *false* otherwise.

Let us write a program to demonstrate the usage of comparison operators:

```rust
//Comparison operators Demo
fn main () {
    //Declare and initialize some variables
    let a = 10;
    let b = 60;
    let c:f64;
    let d:f64;
    c = 7.89;
    d = -4.42;
    //Print a b c d
    println!("\na = {} b = {}\nc = {} d = {}", a, b, c, d);
    //Print results of comparison
    println!("\n\na > b: {}", (a > b));
    println!("\nd < c: {}", (d < c));
    println!("\na == b: {}", (a == b));
    println!("\nc != d: {}", (c != d));
    println!("\na <= b: {}", (a <= b));
    println!("\nd >= c: {}", (d >= c));
}
```

Output:

```
F:\Rust>rustc comparisonoperators.rs
F:\Rust>comparisonoperators.exe
a = 10 b = 60
c = 7.89 d = -4.42

a > b: false
d < c: true
a == b: false
c != d: true
a <= b: true
d >= c: false
F:\Rust>
```

8.3 Logical Operators

Logical Operators are used to carry out logical operations such as **AND, OR** and **NOT**. These operators are used heavily in control structures.

Operator	Description	Sample Usage	Explanation
&&	Logical AND	(Expression 1) && (Expression 2)	Returns *true* if all the operands/expressions are *true*. Returns *false* if any one of the operands/expressions is *false*.
||	Logical OR	(Expression 1) && (Expression 2)	Returns *true* if any of the operands/expressions is *true*. Returns *false* if all of the operands/expressions are *false*.
!	Logical NOT	!(Expression 1)	Inverts the value of the given operand. If the operand is *true*, *false* will be returned and if the operand is *false*, *true* will be returned.

Logical operators are very useful when it comes to combining two or more boolean expressions. Here is a program that shows just that:

```
fn main() {

  let x:isize = 23;
  let y:isize = 44;
  const Z:isize = 23;

  println!("\nx = {} y = {} Z = {}\n", x, y, Z);
  println!("\n(x == y): {}", (x == y));
  println!("\n(x == Z): {}", (x == Z));
  println!("\n(x < y): {}", (x < y));
  println!("\n(Z > x): {}", (Z > x));
```

```
    //Combine more than one boolean expressions using
logical operators
    println!("\n\n(x == y) || (Z != y): {}", ((x == y)
|| (Z != y)));
    println!("\n(x == Z) && (x > y): {}", ((x == Z) &&
(x > y)));
    println!("\n!(Z > x): {}", !(Z > x));
}
```

Output:

```
F:\Rust>rustc logicaloperators.rs
F:\Rust>logicaloperators.exe
x = 23 y = 44 Z = 23

(x == y): false
(x == Z): true
(x < y): true
(Z > x): false

(x == y) || (Z != y): true
(x == Z) && (x > y): false
!(Z > x): true
F:\Rust>
```

8.4 Bitwise Operators

Bitwise Operators work on individual bits of the operands; hence the name. Operations will be carried out in a bit-by-bit manner. In order to understand the working of bitwise operators, some knowledge of boolean algebra and binary number system are needed.

8. Operators

Operator	Description	Sample Usage	Explanation
&	Bitwise Logical AND	x & y	Performs bitwise logical *AND*.
|	Bitwise Logical OR	x | y	Performs bitwise logical *OR*.
^	Bitwise Logical XOR	x ^ y	Performs bitwise logical *XOR*.
<<	Left Shift	x << y	Bits of left operand will be left shifted by the number of times specified by the right operand. For example, *x << 2* will left shift *x's* bits *2 times*.
>>	Right Shift	x >> y	Bits of left operand will be right shifted by the number of times specified by the right operand. For example, *y >> 4* will right shift *y's* bits *4 times*.

Let us write a Rust program to see how bitwise operators work:

```rust
fn main() {
    let x:isize = 5;
    let y:isize = 11;
    println!("\nx = {} y = {}\n", x, y);
    println!("\n(x | y): {}", (x | y));
    println!("\n(x & y): {}", (x & y));
    println!("\n(x ^ y): {}", (x ^ y));
    println!("\n(x << 3): {}", (x << 3));
    println!("\n(y >> 1): {}", (y >> 1));
}
```

Output:

```
C:\Windows\system32\cmd.exe
F:\Rust>rustc bitwiseoperators.rs
F:\Rust>bitwiseoperators.exe
x = 5 y = 11
(x | y): 15
(x & y): 1
(x ^ y): 14
(x << 3): 40
(y >> 1): 5
F:\Rust>
```

8.5 Compound Assignment Operators

The de-facto assignment operator (=) assigns the value on the right to the operand on the left. There are a few more types of assignment operators that allow you to carry out an operation prior to assignment.

Operator	Description	Sample Usage	Equivalent To
+=	Perform arithmetic addition, then assign sum to the operand on the left.	x += y	x = x + y
-=	Subtract operand on the right from the operand on the left and assign difference to the operand on the left.	x -= y	x = x - y
*=	Multiply operands and assign product to the operand on the left.	x *= y	x = x * y
/=	Divide the operand on the left by the operand on the right and assign quotient to the operand on the left.	x /= y	x = x / y

8. Operators

%=	Divide the operand on the left by the operand on the right and assign the arithmetic remainder to the operand on the left.	x %= y	x = x % y
&=	Perform Bitwise Logical AND, assign result to the operand on the left.	x &= y	x = x & y
|=	Perform Bitwise Logical OR, assign result to the operand on the left.	x |= y	x = x | y
^=	Perform Bitwise Logical XOR, assign result to the operand on the left.	x ^= y	x = x ^ y
<<=	Perform left shift, assign result to the operand on the left.	x <<= y	x = x << y
>>=	Perform right shift, assign result to the operand on the left.	x >>= y	x = x >> y

Here is a Rust program that demonstrates the working of compound assignment operators:

```rust
//Compound Assignment Operators
fn main() {
    //Declare some variables
    let mut a:isize = -54;
    let mut b:isize = 73;
    let mut x:f64 = -3.87;
    let mut y:f64 = 4.29;
    //Print everything
    println!("\na = {} b = {} \n\nx = {} y = {}", a, b, x, y);
    a += b;
    println!("\na = {} after performing a += b", a);
    b -= a;
    println!("\nb = {} after performing b -= a", b);
    x *= y;
    println!("\nx = {} after performing x *= y", x);
    y /= x;
```

49

```rust
    println!("\ny = {} after performing y /= x", y);
    a %= b;
    println!("\na = {} after performing a %= b", a);
    a |= b;
    println!("\na = {} after performing a |= b", a);
    a ^= b;
    println!("\na = {} after performing a ^= b", a);
    a <<= 3;
    println!("\na = {} after performing a <<= 3", a);
    a &= b;
    println!("\na = {} after performing a &= b", a);
    b >>= 2;
    println!("\nb = {} after performing b >>= 2", b);
}
```

Output:

```
F:\Rust>rustc compassign.rs
F:\Rust>compassign.exe
a = -54 b = 73
x = -3.87 y = 4.29
a = 19 after performing a += b
b = 54 after performing b -= a
x = -16.6023 after performing x *= y
y = -0.2583979328165375 after performing y /= x
a = 19 after performing a %= b
a = 55 after performing a != b
a = 1 after performing a ^= b
a = 8 after performing a <<= 3
a = 0 after performing a &= b
b = 13 after performing b >>= 2
F:\Rust>
```

9. Type Casting

Type casting is a process of converting data from one type to another. It can also be referred to as *type conversion* but type casting sounds more accurate as type conversion is a broader topic which involves many different concepts. Before going into this topic, let us first understand the need for type casting. Let us consider an arithmetic division example – In *Section 8.1 Notes*, we learned that if an integer is divided by another integer, the quotient will also be an integer. If mathematically, the quotient should have been a float, its fractional component will be discarded and only the integer component will be considered. Here is this concept in action:

```
fn main() {

    let a:isize = 24;
    let b:isize = 5;

    let q = a/b;

    println!("\na = {} \nb = {}\nq = {}\n", a, b, q);
}
```

Output:

```
F:\Rust>rustc divint.rs
F:\Rust>divint.exe
a = 24
b = 5
q = 4
F:\Rust>
```

As seen from the above output, we divide 24 by 5. The quotient should have been 4.8 but we see just 4. It is clear that the fractional part has been discarded.

This is just one example why we need type conversion. There could be many different use cases where you may have to use this concept. Let us now take a look at how to perform type conversion or type casting:

The **as** keyword is used to type cast using the following general syntax:

<variable/constant> as <data type>

Example:

let a:isize = 60;

let b:f64 = a as f64;

let c:f64;

c = (a as f64) * 3.733;

Let us now modify the previous program to make sure that the quotient is a floating point value:

```
//Integer division - Float quotient
fn main() {
    //Declare some variables
    let a:isize = 24;
    let b:isize = 5;
    //Type cast a and b as f64 and then divide
    let q:f64 = (a as f64) / (b as f64);
    //Print everything
    println!("\na = {} \nb = {}\nq = {}\n", a, b, q);
}
```

9. Type Casting

Output:

```
F:\Rust>rustc divint.rs
F:\Rust>divint.exe
a = 24
b = 5
q = 4.8

F:\Rust>
```

Note:

- Not every type can be converted to every other type. For example, a floating point variable has an integer part and a fractional part. If you try to convert a float value to an integer one, the compiler will return an error.

- Type casting can only work with primitive data types. For example, it is not possible to cast an integer (i32) in to a string (&str).

- An integer quotient resulting from an integer division as shown in one of the programs in this chapter is not necessarily a problem. In fact, it is quite useful in many different situations. The said example has been considered only for demonstration purpose.

10. User Input

In this chapter, we will learn how to interact with the user. All of the programming examples that we have seen till the previous chapter had pre-defined hard coded values. None of those examples had any statements that accepted input from the user.

Input can be read from the standard input stream (***stdin***). Streams are logical interconnected communication channels using which a program can read or write data. For convenience, we can consider that keyboard input can be read using the standard input stream. A mutable string of object type is needed to read the input. An object type string can be declared as follows:

let mut <string var> = String::new();

Example:

let mut user_input = String::new();

User input can be read into the object type string with the help of the ***read_line*** function belonging to the I/O module (***io***) of the Rust Standard Library (***std***). Use the following syntax:

std::io::stdin().read_line(&mut <mutable object type string variable>).unwrap();

Example:

std::io::stdin().read_line(&mut user_input).unwrap();

The above statement is a blocking I/O operation. When the execution control encounters this statement, the execution of the program will halt and give an opportunity to the user to enter something through the keyboard and press Enter. Only when the user does so, the program will proceed. If the user does not enter anything, the program will wait there indefinitely unless it is terminated externally.

Let us write a program to accept an input from the user and print it back:

```rust
//User Input Demo
fn main(){
    //Declare a mutable string to store the input
    let mut text = String::new();
    //Prompt the user to enter something
    println!("\nEnter some text :");
    //Read the input using stdin
    std::io::stdin().read_line(&mut text).unwrap();
    //Print whatever was read
    println!("\nYou have entered: {}", text);
}
```

Output:

```
F:\Rust>rustc userinput1.rs
F:\Rust>userinput1.exe
Enter some text :
Hello! This is a sample input.
You have entered: Hello! This is a sample input.

F:\Rust>
```

Note:

- Whatever the user enters through the keyboard will be returned as an object type string only. Even if numbers are entered, they will be read and treated as strings.

10. User Input

- The statement *std::io::stdin().read_line(&mut <mutable object type string variable>).unwrap();* returns the number of bytes read from the stdin. A variable can be used to receive the number of bytes read as follows:

let <var> = std::io::stdin().read_line(&mut <mutable object type string variable>).unwrap();

Example:

let size = std::io::stdin().read_line(&mut user_input).unwrap();

This is completely optional but can be useful in certain situations.

10.1 Reading Numbers

As we have learned that even if the user enters a number, it will be treated as a string; the input needs to be essentially converted to the numerical data type in order for it to be treated as a number. This can be done using a method called parsing. In general programming terms, parsing a string means reading and analysing a string to extract meaningful data. Here is the general syntax to do it:

let <number variable>: <numerical data type> = <string variable>.trim().parse().unwrap();

Example:

let num: i32 = user_input.trim().parse().unwrap();

Note: This method will only work correctly when the user enters a numeric value. If the user enters something other than a number, and you try to parse it in order to convert it to an integer, you will get a runtime error (also known as an exception).

Let us write a program to prompt the user to enter two numbers. We will first store these numbers into object type string variables, convert them into integers, add them and print their sum:

```rust
//User Input Demo - Numbers
fn main(){
    //Declare mutable strings to store the input in string form
    let mut num1_str = String::new();
    let mut num2_str = String::new();
    //Prompt the user to enter a number
    println!("\nEnter a number :");
    //Read the input using stdin, store the string input in num1_str
    std::io::stdin().read_line(&mut num1_str).unwrap();
    //Prompt the user to enter a number
    println!("\nEnter another number :");
    //Read the input using stdin, store the string input in num2_str
    std::io::stdin().read_line(&mut num2_str).unwrap();
    //Parse the input and try to convert string equivalent numbers to int
    let num1: isize = num1_str.trim().parse().unwrap();
    let num2: isize = num2_str.trim().parse().unwrap();
    //Add both numbers
    let sum: isize = num1 + num2;
    //Print num1 num2 and sum
    println!("\nnum1 = {} , num2 = {} \nsum = {}\n", num1, num2, sum);
}
```

10. User Input

Output:

```
F:\Rust>rustc addtwonumbers.rs
F:\Rust>addtwonumbers.exe
Enter a number :
124
Enter another number :
548
num1 = 124 , num2 = 548
sum = 672
F:\Rust>
```

Let us write another program to read float values (f64). We will read two float numbers, multiply them and print their product:

```
fn main(){

    let mut num1_str = String::new();
    let mut num2_str = String::new();

    println!("\nEnter a floating point number :");

    std::io::stdin().read_line(&mut num1_str).unwrap();

    println!("\nEnter another floating point number :");

    std::io::stdin().read_line(&mut num2_str).unwrap();

    let num1: f64 = num1_str.trim().parse().unwrap();
    let num2: f64 = num2_str.trim().parse().unwrap();

    let prod: f64 = num1 * num2;
```

```
    println!("\nnum1 = {} , num2 = {} \nprod = {}\n",
num1, num2, prod);
    }
```

Output:

```
F:\Rust>rustc multiplytwonumbers.rs
F:\Rust>multiplytwonumbers.exe
Enter a floating point number :
-34.65
Enter another floating point number :
19.73

num1 = -34.65 , num2 = 19.73
prod = -683.6445

F:\Rust>
```

11. Decision Making

The topics we have covered so far had programs that execute in a linear manner. That is, a program would begin executing from the first line of the main function till the last one. In programming, ***control structures*** are used to introduce conditionality and exercise more control over the flow of execution of the program. In Rust, control structures are available in the form of decision making constructs and loops. In this chapter, we will cover decision making constructs and loops in the next one. ***If-Else*** and ***Match*** constructs are used to make decisions in Rust.

11.1 if-else Construct

A simplest form of a decision making construct can be realized using a single ***if block***. Here is the general syntax:

if <condition> {

   // Statements to be executed if <condition> is true

}

Example:

if (year > 2000) {

println!("\nIt's the 21st century!");

}

An ***if statement*** should be given a condition marked by ***<condition>*** in the above code snippet. This condition is usually a boolean expression that evaluates to either ***true*** or ***false***. When the execution control encounters an if statement, the given condition will be evaluated. If the condition evaluates to true, the statements inside the if block (enclosed within curly brackets {}) will be executed one by one. Whereas, if the condition evaluates to false, the if block will be skipped and the execution control will move the statement after the end of the if block (if present).

Here is a programming example which contains a single if block:

```
//If demo -- odd or even
fn main(){
    //Declare mutable string to store the input in string form
    let mut num_str = String::new();
    //Prompt the user to enter a number
    println!("\nEnter a number :");
    //Read the input using stdin, store the string input in num_str
    std::io::stdin().read_line(&mut num_str).unwrap();
    //Parse the input and try to convert string equivalent numbers to int
    let num: isize = num_str.trim().parse().unwrap();
    //Check if the number is greater than 10
    if num > 10 {
        println!("\n{} is greater than 10.\n", num);
    }
}
```

11. Decision Making

Output:

```
F:\Rust>rustc ifdemo.rs
F:\Rust>ifdemo.exe
Enter a number :
15
15 is greater than 10.

F:\Rust>ifdemo.exe
Enter a number :
5
F:\Rust>
```

In the above example, there is only one if statement which checks whether a given number is greater than 10. If so, it prints a message and if not, the program does not do anything. Hence when 5 is entered, you do not see anything significant in the above image. If you want to do something if the given condition of the if block fails, you can have an else block following the if block. Here is the general syntax:

if <condition> {

// Statements to be executed if <condition> is true

}

else {

// Statements to be executed if <condition> is false

}

Example:

if (year > 2000) {

println!("\nIt's the 21st century!");

63

}

else {

println!("\nIt's not the 21st century!");

}

Let us write a Rust program to check if the given number is odd or even:

```rust
//If/Else demo -- odd or even
fn main(){
    //Declare mutable string to store the input in string form
    let mut num_str = String::new();
    //Prompt the user to enter a number
    println!("\nEnter a number :");
    //Read the input using stdin, store the string input in num_str
    std::io::stdin().read_line(&mut num_str).unwrap();
    //Parse the input and try to convert string equivalent numbers to int
    let num: isize = num_str.trim().parse().unwrap();
    //Divide num by two, check if the remainder is 1, which means the number is odd
    if num % 2 == 1 {
        println!("\n{} is odd.\n", num);
    }
    //If the remainder is zero, means the number is even
    else {
        println!("\n{} is even.\n", num);
    }
}
```

Output:

```
F:\Rust>rustc oddeven.rs
F:\Rust>oddeven.exe
Enter a number :
7
7 is odd.

F:\Rust>oddeven.exe
Enter a number :
128
128 is even.

F:\Rust>_
```

One combination of if-else blocks can be used to test the validity of one condition – do something if valid and do something else if invalid. If you want to test multiple conditions, you can use multiple else if blocks sandwiched between the if-block and the else block where each else if statement will have a condition of its own. Here is the general syntax:

if <condition 1> {

//Statements to be executed if <condition 1> is true

}

else if <condition 2> {

//Statements to be executed if <condition 1> is false and <condition 2> is true

}

else if <condition 3> {

//Statements to be executed if <condition 1> and <condition 2> are false and <condition 3> is true

}

...

...

...

else {

  //Statements to be executed if all conditions are false

}

Example:

if (year > 2000) {

  println!("\nIt's the 21st century!");

}

else if (year >1900) {

  println!("\nIt's the 20th century!");

}

else if (year >1800) {

  println!("\nIt's the 19th century!");

}

else {

  println!("\nIt's not the 19th, 20th or the 21st century!");

}

11. Decision Making

Let us see this concept in action using a programming example. We will check if the given number is positive, negative or zero:

```rust
fn main(){
    let mut num_str = String::new();
    println!("\nEnter a number :");
    std::io::stdin().read_line(&mut num_str).unwrap();
    let num: isize = num_str.trim().parse().unwrap();
    if num > 0 {
        println!("\n{} is positive.\n", num);
    }
    else if num < 0 {
        println!("\n{} is negative.\n", num);
    }
    else {
        println!("\n{} is zero.\n", num);
    }
}
```

Output:

```
F:\Rust>rustc pnz.rs
F:\Rust>pnz.exe
Enter a number :
0
0 is zero.

F:\Rust>pnz.exe
Enter a number :
-242
-242 is negative.

F:\Rust>pnz.exe
Enter a number :
9873
9873 is positive.

F:\Rust>
```

Multiple conditions can be combined using logical operators. Let us write a program to read an integer from the user and determine in which 10 number range does it belong starting from 1-10, 11-20, ... 91-100:

```rust
//Multiple boolean expression demo -- number within 10 step range
fn main(){
    //Declare mutable string to store the input in string form
    let mut num_str = String::new();
    //Prompts the user to enter a number
    println!("\nEnter a number between 1 and 100 : ");
    //Read the input using stdin, store the string input in num_str
    std::io::stdin().read_line(&mut num_str).unwrap();
    //Parse the input and try to convert string equivalent numbers to int
    let num: isize = num_str.trim().parse().unwrap();
    //Check which range does num belong to
    if (num > 0) && (num <= 10) {
```

11. Decision Making

```
        println!("\n{} is in the range of ONE to TEN\n", num);
    }
    else if (num > 10) && (num <= 20) {
        println!("\n{} is in the range of ELEVEN to TWENTY\n", num);
    }
    else if (num > 20) && (num <= 30) {
        println!("\n{} is in the range of TWENTY ONE to THIRTY\n", num);
    }
    else if (num > 30) && (num <= 40) {
        println!("\n{} is in the range of THIRTY ONE to FORTY\n", num);
    }
    else if (num > 40) && (num <= 50) {
        println!("\n{} is in the range of FORTY ONE to FIFTY\n", num);
    }
    else if (num > 50) && (num <= 60) {
        println!("\n{} is in the range of FIFTY ONE to SIXTY\n", num);
    }
    else if (num > 60) && (num <= 70) {
        println!("\n{} is in the range of SIXTY ONE to SEVENTY\n", num);
    }
    else if (num > 70) && (num <= 80) {
        println!("\n{} is in the range of SEVENTY ONE to EIGHTY\n", num);
    }
    else if (num > 80) && (num <= 90) {
        println!("\n{} is in the range of EIGHTY ONE to NINETY\n", num);
    }
    else if (num > 90) && (num <= 100) {
```

```
        println!("\n{} is in the range of NINETY ONE to HUNDRED\n", num);
    }
    else {
        println!("\n{} is either less than ONE or greater than ONE HUNDRED\n", num);
    }
}
```

Output:

```
F:\Rust>rustc numinrange.rs
F:\Rust>numinrange.exe
Enter a number between 1 and 100 :
51
51 is in the range of FIFTY ONE to SIXTY

F:\Rust>numinrange.exe
Enter a number between 1 and 100 :
-4
-4 is either less than ONE or greater than ONE HUNDRED

F:\Rust>numinrange.exe
Enter a number between 1 and 100 :
1093
1093 is either less than ONE or greater than ONE HUNDRED

F:\Rust>numinrange.exe
Enter a number between 1 and 100 :
75
75 is in the range of SEVENTY ONE to EIGHTY

F:\Rust>
```

Note:

- An if statement can be stand-alone but else-if and else statements need a preceding if statement to work.

- An if block should be immediately followed by either an else-if block or an else block. No other statements are permitted between blocks.

- When there is an if block and multiple else-if blocks; when there are multiple conditions which can evaluate to true, only the first block with a true condition will be executed and rest of the blocks will be ignored as the control moves forward in a sequential manner.

11.2 match Construct

If -Else If – Else supports accept boolean expressions. A boolean expression can evaluate to either true or false. If it evaluates to true, you can do something and if it evaluates to false, you can do something else. A match construct allows you to use an expression which can evaluate to anything, not just true or false. This is similar to the switch-case construct seen in programming languages such as C/C++, Java, C#, etc. Here is the general syntax:

match ([expression]) {

[MatchArm 1 - Constant Expression 1] => { //Statements to be executed if [expression] matches [Constant Expression 1] is matched },

[MatchArm 2 - Constant Expression 2] => { //Statements to be executed if [expression] matches [Constant Expression 2] is matched },

[MatchArm 3 - Constant Expression 3] => { //Statements to be executed if [expression] matches [Constant Expression 3] is matched },

...

...

...

[MatchArm n - Constant Expression n] => { //*Statements to be executed if [expression] matches [Constant Expression n] is matched* }

_ => { //*Statements to be executed if [expression] matches none of the constant expressions*}

};

The match statement should be given an expression marked by *[expression]* in the above code snippet. Inside the match block, there are match arms. A match arm is made up of different types of constant expression. When the expression is evaluated, the execution control tries to find a matching constant expression by going through the match arms sequentially. If a matching expression is found, that match arm is executed. If no matching constant expression is found, the default match arm given by an **underscore (_)** is executed. Let us write a program to accept the serial number of a month from the user and determine which month it is:

```
//Basic Match Demo
fn main(){
    //Declare mutable string to store the input in string form
    let mut month_str = String::new();
    //Prompt the user to enter a number
    println!("\nEnter the months's number (1-12) : ");
    //Read the input using stdin, store the string input in month_str
    std::io::stdin().read_line(&mut month_str).unwrap();
    //Parse the input and try to convert string equivalent numbers to int
    let month: isize = month_str.trim().parse().unwrap();
```

11. Decision Making

```
match month {
    1 => { println!("\nJanuary\n") },
    2 => { println!("\nFebruary\n") },
    3 => { println!("\nMarch\n") },
    4 => { println!("\nApril\n") },
    5 => { println!("\nMay\n") },
    6 => { println!("\nJune\n") },
    7 => { println!("\nJuly\n") },
    8 => { println!("\nAugust\n") },
    9 => { println!("\nSeptember\n") },
    10 => { println!("\nOctober\n") },
    11 => { println!("\nNovember\n") },
    12 => { println!("\nDecember\n") },
    _ => { println!("\nInvalid Input!\n") }
};
}
```

Output:

```
F:\Rust>rustc matchbasic.rs
F:\Rust>matchbasic.exe
Enter the months's number (1-12) :
6
June

F:\Rust>matchbasic.exe
Enter the months's number (1-12) :
0
Invalid Input!

F:\Rust>matchbasic.exe
Enter the months's number (1-12) :
10
October

F:\Rust>
```

A variable can be assigned a value based on the match found using the following syntax of match:

let <variable> = match ([expression]) {

[MatchArm 1 - Constant Expression 1] => {Value to be assigned to <variable> if [expression] matches [Constant Expression 1] },

[MatchArm 2 - Constant Expression 2] => {Value to be assigned to <variable> if [expression] matches [Constant Expression 2] },

[MatchArm 3 - Constant Expression 3] => {Value to be assigned to <variable> if [expression] matches [Constant Expression 3] },

...

...

...

[MatchArm n - Constant Expression n] => [Value to be assigned to <variable> if [expression] matches [Constant Expression n]]

_ => [Value to be assigned to <variable> if no expressions match]

};

Let us write a program to ask the user to enter a single digit (0-9), convert it to words and assign to a string variable:

```rust
//Match Demo
fn main(){
    //Declare mutable string to store the input in string form
    let mut num_str = String::new();
    //Prompt the user to enter a number
    println!("\nEnter a number :");
    //Read the input using stdin, store the string input in num_str
    std::io::stdin().read_line(&mut num_str).unwrap();
    //Parse the input and try to convert string equivalent numbers to int
```

11. Decision Making

```
    let num: isize = num_str.trim().parse().unwrap();
    let num_str = match num {
        0 => "ZERO",
        1 => "ONE",
        2 => "TWO",
        3 => "THREE",
        4 => "FOUR",
        5 => "FIVE",
        6 => "SIX",
        7 => "SEVEN",
        8 => "EIGHT",
        9 => "NINE",
        _ => "An Invalid Input!"
    };
    println!("\nYou have entered: {}\n", num_str);
}
```

Output:

```
F:\Rust>rustc matchdemo.rs
F:\Rust>matchdemo.exe
Enter a number :
0
You have entered: ZERO

F:\Rust>matchdemo.exe
Enter a number :
15
You have entered: An Invalid Input!

F:\Rust>matchdemo.exe
Enter a number :
5
You have entered: FIVE

F:\Rust>
```

Two or more constant expressions can be separated using the | operator in case the same group of statements need to be executed for multiple matching expressions. Here is a programming example that demonstrates this concept – checks whether a given alphabet is a consonant or a vowel:

```rust
//Match Demo - Multiple Constant Expressions
fn main(){
    //Declare mutable string to store the input in string form
    let mut char_str = String::new();
    //Prompt the user to enter an alphabet
    println!("\nEnter an alphabet :");
    //Read the input using stdin, store the string input in char_str
    std::io::stdin().read_line(&mut char_str).unwrap();
    //Parse the input and try to convert string equivalent numbers to int
    let c: char = char_str.trim().parse().unwrap();
    //Match for c
    match c {
        'a' | 'e' | 'i' | 'o' | 'u' | 'A' | 'E' | 'I' | 'O' | 'U' => { println!("\n{} is a vowel.\n", c)},
        _ => { println!("\n{} is a consonant.\n", c) }
    };
}
```

11. Decision Making

Output:

```
F:\Rust>rustc matchmultiple.rs
F:\Rust>matchmultiple.exe
Enter an alphabet :
Z
Z is a consonant.

F:\Rust>matchmultiple.exe
Enter an alphabet :
e
e is a vowel.

F:\Rust>matchmultiple.exe
Enter an alphabet :
k
k is a consonant.

F:\Rust>matchmultiple.exe
Enter an alphabet :
A
A is a vowel.

F:\Rust>
```

A particular match arm can be activated for a range of values. The range can be specified using the range operator as follows:

[start value]..=[end value] => {//Statements to be executed if the expression evaluates to a value in this range] }

Example:

1900..=2000 => {println!("\nIt is the 20th century!");}

Let us understand this concept with a programming example:

```
fn main(){

    let mut num_str = String::new();

    println!("\nEnter a number between 1 and 1000 : ");
```

```rust
    //Read the input using stdin, store the string
input in num_str
    std::io::stdin().read_line(&mut num_str).unwrap();
    //Parse the input and try to convert string
equivalent numbers to int
    let num: isize = num_str.trim().parse().unwrap();
    //Check which range does num belong to using match
    match num {
        1..=99 => { println!("\n{} is between 1 and 99.\n", num ) },
        100..=199 => { println!("\n{} is between 100 and 199.\n", num ) },
        200..=299 => { println!("\n{} is between 200 and 299.\n", num ) },
        300..=399 => { println!("\n{} is between 300 and 399.\n", num ) },
        400..=499 => { println!("\n{} is between 400 and 499.\n", num) },
        500..=599 => { println!("\n{} is between 500 and 599.\n", num ) },
        600..=699 => { println!("\n{} is between 600 and 699.\n", num ) },
        700..=799 => { println!("\n{} is between 700 and 799.\n", num ) },
        800..=899 => { println!("\n{} is between 800 and 899.\n", num ) },
        900..=1000 => { println!("\n{} is between 900 and 1000.\n", num ) },
        _ => { println!("\n{} is either less than 1 or greater than 1000.\n", num) },
    };
}
```

Output:

```
F:\Rust>rustc matchrange.rs
F:\Rust>matchrange.exe
Enter a number between 1 and 1000 :
501
501 is between 500 and 599.

F:\Rust>matchrange.exe
Enter a number between 1 and 1000 :
0
0 is either less than 1 or greater than 1000.

F:\Rust>matchrange.exe
Enter a number between 1 and 1000 :
4037
4037 is either less than 1 or greater than 1000.

F:\Rust>matchrange.exe
Enter a number between 1 and 1000 :
725
725 is between 700 and 799.

F:\Rust>
```

Note:

- The process of trying to find a matching expression happens sequentially. If there are multiple matching expressions, only that arm with the first matching expression will be executed. Rest of the arms will be ignored.

- It is important to include the default match arm given by underscore. Otherwise, the compiler will return an error.

- Different decision making constructs can be nested within each other.

12. Loops

A loop is a type of control structure that can be used to execute a piece of code over a number of times. Rust offers 3 types of loops – *while, loop (keyword)* and *for.* Let us take a look at each one of these.

12.1 while Loop

A while loop will go on executing as long as a given condition is met. Here is the general syntax:

while <condition> {

//Statements to be executed as long as <condition> is true.

}

Example:

let mut count = 0;

while count < 10 {

print!("\n{}", count);

count = count + 1;

}

As mentioned earlier, there is a condition associated with a while loop marked by ***<condition>*** in the above code snippet. When this condition will be evaluated for the first time, if it returns ***false***, the entire while block will be skipped. If it evaluates to ***true***, the statements inside the while block will be executed one by one till the last statement inside the block. This is known as *one loop iteration*. When the end of block is reached, the execution control will jump back to the beginning of the loop and the condition will be checked again. If it evaluates to true again, the block will be executed once again. This process will go on happening as long as the condition keeps evaluating to true. If the condition never evaluates to false, the loop will run endlessly. Such a loop is known as an *infinite loop*. In the above example, there is a variable called *count* which is initialized to *0*. The condition specified for the while loop is *count < 10*. This means, as long as the value of count remains below 10, the loop block will go on executing. Inside the loop, count is printed using the print! Macro and the next statement is very important where count is incremented by 1. If the value of count does not change, it will remain below 10 forever and the while loop will go on executing forever. Let us consider a programming example which demonstrates the usage of while loop:

```
fn main() {
    let mut count: isize = 1;
    while count <= 10 {
        println!("{}", 2 * count);
        count += 1;
    }
}
```

12. Loops

Output:

```
F:\Rust>rustc whiledemo.rs
F:\Rust>whiledemo.exe
2
4
6
8
10
12
14
16
18
20
F:\Rust>
```

Two loop control statements are available in Rust – *continue* and *break*. When a continue statement is encountered, the current iteration is skipped and the control jumps back to the beginning of the loop. Where as, when break statement is encountered, the execution of the loop stops and the control comes out of the loop.

Let us write a program which prints the multiples of 3 from 3 to 30 but skips multiples of 5. This is done using the *continue* statement:

```
fn main() {

    let mut count: isize = 1;
    let mut multiple;

    while count <= 10 {
        multiple = count * 3;
        if multiple % 5 == 0 {
            count += 1;
            continue;
        }
        println!("{}", multiple);
```

83

```
        count += 1;
    }
}
```

Output:

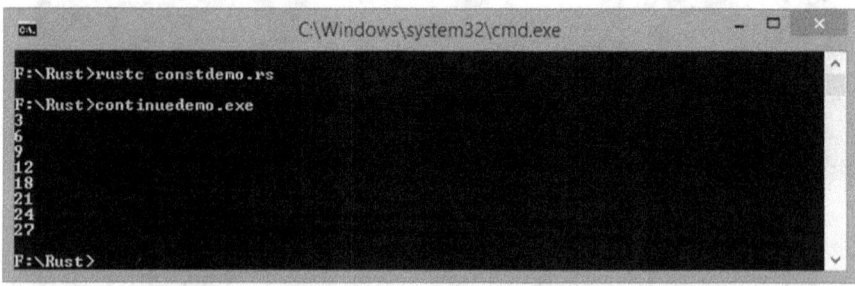

12.2 loop Keyword

The *loop* keyword will keep executing the following loop block enclosed within curly brackets. The only way to terminate this block is using the *break* statement. Here is the general syntax:

loop {

　//Statements to be executed

}

Let us write a program using the loop keyword to print multiples of 5 from 5 to 50:

```
//loop demo
fn main() {
    //Initialize counter to 1
    let mut count: isize = 1;
    //Iterate from 1 to 10
    loop {
        println!("{}", 5 * count);
        count += 1;
        if count == 11 {
```

```
            break;
        }
    }
}
```

Output:

```
F:\Rust>rustc loopdemo.rs
F:\Rust>loopdemo.exe
5
10
15
20
25
30
35
40
45
50
F:\Rust>
```

12.3 for Loop

A for loop only works on Iterators. An Iterators is a programming construct used to iterate through collections like arrays, vectors, etc. One of the simplest ways of realizing a collection is using ranges. Here is the general syntax of using for loop with ranges:

for <element> in <first value of range>..=<last value of range> {

//Statements

}

Example:

for num in 0..=9 {

print!("\n{}", num);

}

In the above example, **num** will hold incremental values from the range 0 to 9. That is, during the first iteration, num will hold the value 0, 1 during the second iteration, 2 during the third iteration and so on. Let us write a program to calculate factorial of a number using for loop:

```rust
//For demo -- factorial
fn main() {
    //Declare mutable string to store the input in string form
    let mut num_str = String::new();
    //Prompt the user to enter a number
    println!("\nEnter a number :");
    //Read the input using stdin, store the string input in num_str
    std::io::stdin().read_line(&mut num_str).unwrap();
    //Parse the input and try to convert string equivalent numbers to int
    let num: isize = num_str.trim().parse().unwrap();
    let mut factorial: isize = 1;
    if num >= 0 {
        for i in 1..=num {
            factorial = factorial * i;
        }
        println!("\nFactorial of {} is {}\n", num, factorial);
    }
    else {
        println!("\nFactorial of a negative number cannot be calculated.\n")
    }
}
```

12. Loops

Output:

```
F:\Rust>rustc factorial.rs
F:\Rust>factorial.exe
Enter a number :
8
Factorial of 8 is 40320

F:\Rust>
```

We know that a string is a sequence of characters. This means that it is a collection of some type. However it does not automatically qualify as an iterator. To do so, you have to use the *chars()* function using the following syntax:

<string variable>.chars()

Example:

for x in name.chars()

{

// Statements

}

During each iteration of the loop in the above example, a character from the string variable *name* will be fetched into *x* in a sequential manner. Let us write a program to print individual characters of a string:

```rust
fn main() {

    let mut str1 = String::new();
```

```
println!("\nEnter something :");
//Read the input using stdin, store the string 
input in str1
std::io::stdin().read_line(&mut str1).unwrap();
for alphabet in str1.chars() {
    print!("\n{}", alphabet);
}
}
```

Output:

```
F:\Rust>rustc fordemo.rs
F:\Rust>fordemo.exe
Enter something :
Hello!
H
e
l
l
o
!
F:\Rust>
```

12.4 Nested Loops

A loop can be nested inside another loop. There is no limit to the level of nesting. There are no hard and fast rules of nesting as such. Let us write a program to generate the following pattern:

0

010

01210

0123210

012343210

01234543210

12. Loops

```rust
fn main() {
    let mut i:isize = 0;
    let mut j:isize;
    let mut k:isize;
    print!("\n");
    loop {
        for _a in i..=5 {
            print!(" ");
        }
        j = 0;
        while j < i {

            print!("{}", j);
            j += 1;
        }
        k = j;
        while k >= 0 {
            print!("{}", k);
            k -= 1;
        }
        i +=1;
        if i == 6 {
            break;
        }
        print!("\n");
    }
    print!("\n");
}
```

Output:

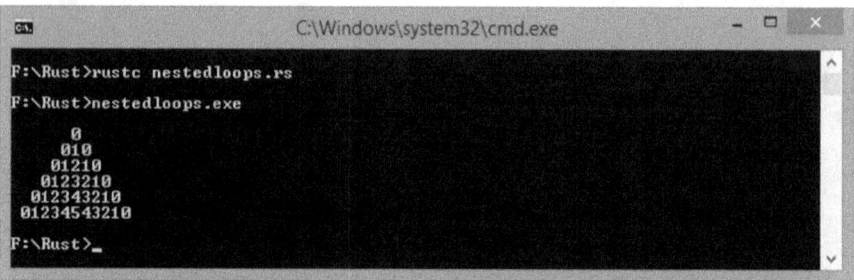

Note: Working with loops can be tricky at first and it is very normal for new programmers to unintentionally write infinite loops. If you happen to do so and if your program gets stuck, you may use the ***CTRL+C*** key combination to interrupt the program or ***CTRL+Z*** key combination to stop the program. Either one of these will work.

13. Arrays

An array is a collection of elements of the same data type. Memory regions for storing the elements of an array are reserved in a sequential manner. Here is the general syntax of declaring an array:

let <array variable> : [<optional data type>; <optional size>] = [<elements separated by comma>]

Example:

let num_array: [i32; 3] = [80, 90, 100];

Elements in an array are present at locations called *indexes*. An array index begins at *0* and ends at *(size – 1)*. In the above example, the element 80 would be present at index 0, 90 will be present at 1 and 100 will be present at index 2 (array size is 3, size - 1 is 2). This is what the array will look like in the memory:

num_array

Data =>	80	90	100
Index =>	0	1	2

When declaring an array, data type and size is optional but the array elements should be of the same data type. For example, the following array declarations are totally valid:

let x_array = [-5.7, 8.9786, 6.0, -3.76, 0.04];

let country = ["USA", "UK", "Australia"];

All the elements of an array can be printed at once using the print and println macros with the help of *{:?}* substitution operator. Let us consider we want to print the contents of **x_array** and ***country***:

println!("x_array: {:?}", x_array);

println!("country: {:?}", country);

Size of an array can be determined with the help of the ***len()*** function. Syntax:

<size variable> = <array_variable>.len();

Example:

size = x_array.len();

An array of default values can be created with the following syntax:

let <array variable>:[<data type>; <size>] = [>default value>; <size>];

Let us write a simple Rust program to declare different types of arrays and print their contents along with their size:

```rust
//Arrays demo - Basic initialize and print
fn main() {
    //Declare integer array
    let num_array = [4, 7, -3, 0, 9];
    //Declare float array, specify type and size
    let fl_array: [f64;5] = [-7.4, 0.3, -5.12, 4.9, 8.3];
    //Declare string array, specify type and size
    let name_array: [&str;7] = ["Alice", "Bob", "Poonam", "Dexter", "Willo", "Ian", "Gera"];
```

13. Arrays

```
    //Fill an integer array of size 3 with value 5
    let num_def_array:[isize;3] = [5;3];
    //Fill a float array of size 4 with value 0.0
    let fl_def_array:[f64;4] = [0.0;4];
    //Fill a string (&str) array of size 7 with value
"NULL"
    let string_def_array:[&str;7] = ["NULL";7];
    //Fill a boolean array of size 5 with value true
    let boolean_def_array:[bool;4] = [true;4];
    //Print everything
    println!("\nnum_array: {:?}", num_array);
    println!("\nnum_array Size: {}", num_array.len());
    println!("\nfl_array: {:?}", fl_array);
    println!("\nfl_array Size: {}", fl_array.len());
    println!("\nname_array: {:?}", name_array);
   println!("\nname_array Size: {}", name_array.len());
    println!("\nnum_def_array: {:?}", num_def_array);
    println!("\nnum_def_array        Size:         {}",
num_def_array.len());
    println!("\nfl_def_array: {:?}", fl_def_array);
    println!("\nfl_def_array        Size:         {}",
fl_def_array.len());
    println!("\nstring_def_array:                {:?}",
string_def_array);
    println!("\ntring_def_array:       Size:        {}",
string_def_array.len());
    println!("\nboolean_def_array:               {:?}",
boolean_def_array);
    println!("\nboolean_def_array      Size:        {}",
boolean_def_array.len());
    }
```

Output:

```
F:\Rust>rustc array1.rs
F:\Rust>array1.exe
num_array: [4, 7, -3, 0, 9]
num_array Size: 5
fl_array: [-7.4, 0.3, -5.12, 4.9, 8.3]
fl_array Size: 5
name_array: ["Alice", "Bob", "Poonam", "Dexter", "Willo", "Ian", "Gera"]
name_array Size: 7
nnum_def_array: [5, 5, 5]
nnum_def_array Size: 3
fl_def_array: [0.0, 0.0, 0.0, 0.0]
fl_def_array Size: 4
string_def_array: ["NULL", "NULL", "NULL", "NULL", "NULL", "NULL", "NULL"]
string_def_array: Size: 7
boolean_def_array: [true, true, true, true]
boolean_def_array Size: 4
F:\Rust>
```

13.1 Accessing Array Elements

Array elements can be accessed using the *access operator* (*[]*). Here is the general syntax:

<array variable>[<index>]

Example:

let x = num[4];

println!("\nElement at index 4: {}", x);

Let us declare an array and print its elements index by index:

```
//Arrays demo - print element by element
fn main() {
    //Declare integer array
    let num_array: [i32;10] = [15, -76, -23, 26, 82, -54, 34, 0, 64, 96];
```

13. Arrays

```
    println!("\nElement at index 0: {}", num_array[0]);
    println!("\nElement at index 1: {}", num_array[1]);
    println!("\nElement at index 2: {}", num_array[2]);
    println!("\nElement at index 3: {}", num_array[3]);
    println!("\nElement at index 4: {}", num_array[4]);
    println!("\nElement at index 5: {}", num_array[5]);
    println!("\nElement at index 6: {}", num_array[6]);
    println!("\nElement at index 7: {}", num_array[7]);
    println!("\nElement at index 8: {}", num_array[8]);
    println!("\nElement at index 9: {}", num_array[9]);
}
```

Output:

```
F:\Rust>rustc array2.rs
F:\Rust>array2.exe
Element at index 0: 15
Element at index 1: -76
Element at index 2: -23
Element at index 3: 26
Element at index 4: 82
Element at index 5: -54
Element at index 6: 34
Element at index 7: 0
Element at index 8: 64
Element at index 9: 96
F:\Rust>
```

Elements of an array can also be modified by specifying the index; but this will only work if the array has been declared as mutable using the ***mut*** keyword. Here is a program where we create a float array, modify its elements and then print it back:

```
fn main() {
```

```rust
    let mut num_array_f: [f64;5] = [1.67, -8.45, 3.76, -5.19, 7.31];
    //print original array
    println!("\nnum_array_f: {:?}", num_array_f);
    //Change elements of num_array_f
    num_array_f[0] = 0.0;
    num_array_f[1] = 6.09;
    num_array_f[2] = 1.73;
    num_array_f[3] = 8.23;
    num_array_f[4] = 2.22;
    //print original array
    println!("\nnum_array_f (after modification): {:?}", num_array_f);
}
```

Output:

```
F:\Rust>rustc array3.rs
F:\Rust>array3.exe
num_array_f: [1.67, -8.45, 3.76, -5.19, 7.31]
num_array_f (after modification): [0.0, 6.09, 1.73, 8.23, 2.22]
F:\Rust>
```

13.2 Arrays and Loops

We know that array indexes are assigned in a sequential manner. This means we can easily access array elements using loops. If using while loop or the loop keyword, the loop counter variable should be initialized to 0 and the loop should be run till size – 1. Here is a program that uses a while loop to access an array:

```rust
//Arrays demo - while loop
fn main() {
    //Declare string array, specify type and size
```

```rust
    let name_array: [&str;6] = ["Theo", "Nina", "Eva", "Otis", "Vin", "Sidi"];

    let mut count = 0;
    println!("\nname_array    printed    using    while loop:\n");

    while count < name_array.len() {
        println!("\nElement   at    {}:    {}", count, name_array[count]);

        count = count + 1;
    }

    println!("\n\nArray size: {}\n", count);
}
```

Output:

```
C:\Windows\system32\cmd.exe

F:\Rust>rustc array4.rs
F:\Rust>array4.exe
name_array printed using while loop:

Element at 0: Theo
Element at 1: Nina
Element at 2: Eva
Element at 3: Otis
Element at 4: Vin
Element at 5: Sidi

Array size: 6
```

A for loop can also be used to access the elements of an array. We know that for loop only works on iterators. An array is a collection but that does not make it an iterator by default. However, you can use the ***iter()*** function to convert an array to an iterator using the following syntax:

for <variable> in <array_variable>.iter() {

// Statements

}

Example:

for x in num.iter() {

print!("\n{}", x);

}

Let us write a Rust program to access a string array using a for loop:

```rust
//Arrays demo - for loop with arrays
fn main() {
    //Declare string array, specify type and size
    let city_array: [&str;5] = ["Taipei", "Casablanca", "Oslo", "Santiago", "Waterloo"];
    println!("\ncity_array printed using for loop:\n");
    for city in city_array.iter() {
        println!("\n{}", city);
    }
    println!("\n");
}
```

13. Arrays

Output:

```
F:\Rust>rustc array5.rs
F:\Rust>array5.exe
city_array printed using for loop:

Taipei
Casablanca
Oslo
Santiago
Waterloo

F:\Rust>
```

Let us now take a programming example that combines many different concepts. We will create an array of integers with 0 as the default value. We will then ask the user to enter 5 values, put those in to the number array. Further, calculate the sum and average of those 5 elements:

```
fn main(){

    let mut num_str = String::new();

    let mut i = 0;

    let mut sum:isize = 0;
    let avg:f64;

    let mut num_array: [isize;5] = [0;5];

    while i < 5 {

        println!("\nEnter a number at index {}: ", i);
```

99

```rust
        //Clear num_str so that previous input is flushed
        num_str.clear();
        //Read the input using stdin, store the string input in num_str
        std::io::stdin().read_line(&mut num_str).unwrap();
        //Parse the input and try to convert string equivalent numbers to int
        //Place it into an array
        num_array[i] = num_str.trim().parse().unwrap();
        //Add current element to sum
        sum = sum + num_array[i];
        //Increment i
        i += 1;
    }
    //Calculate average
    avg = (sum as f64) / 5.0;
    //Print everything
    println!("\nnum_array: {:?}", num_array);
    println!("\nnum_array Size: {}", num_array.len());
    println!("\nSum of elements: {}", sum);
    println!("\nAverage: {}", avg);
}
```

13. Arrays

Output:

```
F:\Rust>rustc sumavgarr.rs
F:\Rust>sumavgarr.exe
Enter a number at index 0:
8
Enter a number at index 1:
-2
Enter a number at index 2:
5
Enter a number at index 3:
-3
Enter a number at index 4:
9
num_array: [8, -2, 5, -3, 9]
num_array Size: 5
Sum of elements: 17
Average: 3.4
F:\Rust>
```

Let us consider another practical example where we will ask the user to enter 5 integers, put them in the array and determine the greatest element:

```rust
fn main(){

    let mut num_str = String::new();

    let mut i = 0;

    let mut greatest:isize = -999;

    let mut num_array: [isize;5] = [0;5];

    while i < 5 {

        println!("\nEnter a number at index {}: ", i);
```

```rust
        num_str.clear();
        //Read the input using stdin, store the string input in num_str
        std::io::stdin().read_line(&mut num_str).unwrap();
        //Parse the input and try to convert string equivalent numbers to int
        //Place it into an array
        num_array[i] = num_str.trim().parse().unwrap();
        //Check if the current number is greater than greatest
        if num_array[i] > greatest {
            //Assign greatest to current element
            greatest = num_array[i];
        }
        //Increment i
        i += 1;
    }
    //Print array and greatest
    println!("\nnum_array:    {:?}    \nGreatest:    {}", num_array, greatest);
}
```

Output:

```
F:\Rust>rustc greatest.rs
F:\Rust>greatest.exe
Enter a number at index 0:
67
Enter a number at index 1:
-23
Enter a number at index 2:
88
Enter a number at index 3:
-36
Enter a number at index 4:
12
num_array: [67, -23, 88, -36, 12]
Greatest: 88
F:\Rust>
```

13.3 Array Slices

An array slice is a reference to a part of the array. Can also be considered as a "view" into the array. Here is a general syntax to slice an array:

<slice variable> = &<array variable>[<start index>..<end index>];

Example:

let x = &num[2..9];

In the above example, **x** is an array slice containing elements of **num** from index **2** to **9**. Let us write a Rust program to declare multiple arrays and the corresponding slices:

```
fn main() {

  let num_array = [5, 9, 1, 0, 4, 2, 1, 8];

  let fl_array: [f64;4] = [11.2, 87.4, 91.6, 32.5];

  let country_array: [&str;5] = ["India", "Greece", "Thailand", "Armenia", "Ukraine"];

  let num_slice = &num_array[2..6];

  let fl_slice = &fl_array[1..3];

  let country_slice = &country_array[0..4];

  println!("\nnum_array: {:?} \nnum_array Size: {}\n", num_array, num_array.len());
  println!("\nfl_array: {:?} \nfl_array Size: {}\n", fl_array, fl_array.len());
```

```
    println!("\ncountry_array:    {:?}   \ncountry_array
Size: {}\n", country_array, country_array.len());
    println!("\nnum_slice: {:?} \nnum_slice Size: {}\n",
num_slice, num_slice.len());
    println!("\nfl_slice: {:?} \nfl_slice Size: {}\n",
fl_slice, fl_slice.len());
    println!("\ncountry_slice:    {:?}   \ncountry_slice
Size: {}\n", country_slice, country_slice.len());
}
```

Output:

```
F:\Rust>rustc arrayslice.rs
F:\Rust>arrayslice.exe
num_array: [5, 9, 1, 0, 4, 2, 1, 8]
num_array Size: 8

fl_array: [11.2, 87.4, 91.6, 32.5]
fl_array Size: 4

country_array: ["India", "Greece", "Thailand", "Armenia", "Ukraine"]
country_array Size: 5

num_slice: [1, 0, 4, 2]
num_slice Size: 4

fl_slice: [87.4, 91.6]
fl_slice Size: 2

country_slice: ["India", "Greece", "Thailand", "Armenia"]
country_slice Size: 4

F:\Rust>
```

It is worth noting that a slice cannot exist on its own because it is just a reference to an array; it does not have a memory regions assigned for it. Other than that, a slice behaves just like an array for the most part. For example, you can use the *len()* function on a slice, use loops to access the elements (use *iter()* function when using for loop), and so on. Here is an example where we access slices using loops:

13. Arrays

```rust
fn main() {

    let num_array = [10, 45, 0, 24, 75, 12];

    let fl_array = [-5.7, -9.6, 5.8, 1.3, 4.5];

    let num_slice = &num_array[0..3];
    let fl_slice = &fl_array[1..4];

    println!("\nnum_array: {:?} \nnum_array Size: {}\n", num_array, num_array.len());
    println!("\nnum_slice    (ref    &num_array[0..3]) printed using while loop: \n");
    let mut i = 0;
    while i < num_slice.len() {
        println!("Element at slice index {}: {}", i, num_slice[i]);
        i = i + 1;
    }
    println!("\nfl_array: {:?} \nfl_array Size: {}\n", fl_array, fl_array.len());
    println!("\nfl_slice (ref &fl_array[1..4]) printed using for loop: \n");
    for element in fl_slice {
        println!("{}", element);
    }
    println!();
}
```

Output:

```
F:\Rust>rustc sliceloop.rs

F:\Rust>sliceloop.exe
num_array: [10, 45, 0, 24, 75, 12]
num_array Size: 6

num_slice (ref &num_array[0..3]) printed using while loop:

Element at slice index 0: 10
Element at slice index 1: 45
Element at slice index 2: 0

fl_array: [-5.7, -9.6, 5.8, 1.3, 4.5]
fl_array Size: 5

fl_slice (ref &fl_array[1..4]) printed using for loop:
-9.6
5.8
1.3

F:\Rust>
```

14. Vectors

Similar to an array, a vector (written as *Vec<t>*) is a data structure that is a collection of similar items with one major difference – the size of a vector can increase, thus allowing for more items to be added while the size of an array remains fixed after declaration. Vectors can be referred to as growable arrays. The implementation and methods to work on vectors lie in the *Vec* module of the Rust standard library – *std::Vec*. A vector can be defined using the *vec!* macro as follows:

let <vector variable> = vec![<element 1>, <element 2>, ... <element n>];

Example:

let str = vec!["hello", "how", "are", "you];

Let us write a program to create vectors of different data types:

```
fn main() {

    let num_vector = vec![-5, 8, 0, -2, 9];

    let fl_vector = vec![4.6, 0.5, 7.3];

    let name_vector =    vec!["Dexter",   "Jerry", "Courage"];

    println!("\nnum_vector: {:?}", num_vector);
    println!("\nnum_vector Size: {}", num_vector.len());
    println!("\nfl_vector: {:?}", fl_vector);
```

```
    println!("\nfl_vector Size: {}", fl_vector.len());
    println!("\nname_vector: {:?}", name_vector);
    println!("\nname_vector Size: {}", name_vector.len());
}
```

Output:

```
F:\Rust>rustc vector1.rs
F:\Rust>vector1.exe
num_vector: [-5, 8, 0, -2, 9]
num_vector Size: 5
fl_vector: [4.6, 0.5, 7.3]
fl_vector Size: 3
name_vector: ["Dexter", "Jerry", "Courage"]
name_vector Size: 3
F:\Rust>
```

Individual elements of a vector can be accessed by specifying the index as follows:

<element variable> = <vector variable>[<index>];

Example:

let first = name[0];

let last = name[9];

Let us write a program to access individual elements of a vector:

```
//Vector demo - print element by element
fn main() {
    //Declare integer vector
    let num_vector = vec![34, -65, 77, 12, -23, 85];
    //print value at each index
    println!("\nElement at index 0: {}", num_vector[0]);
    println!("\nElement at index 1: {}", num_vector[1]);
```

```
    println!("\nElement at index 2: {}", num_vector[2]);
    println!("\nElement at index 3: {}", num_vector[3]);
    println!("\nElement at index 4: {}", num_vector[4]);
    println!("\nElement at index 5: {}", num_vector[5]);
}
```

Output:

```
F:\Rust>rustc vector2.rs
F:\Rust>vector2.exe
Element at index 0: 34
Element at index 1: -65
Element at index 2: 77
Element at index 3: 12
Element at index 4: -23
Element at index 5: 85
F:\Rust>
```

Element at an index can be changed using the following syntax as long as the vector has been declared as mutable:

<vector variable>[<index>] = <value> / <variable> / <expression>;

Example:

city[3] = "New Delhi";

Loops can also be used to access the elements of a vector. It is even convenient to use a for loop as vectors are iterators by default. Here is a program that uses while loop and for loop to access elements of different vectors:

```
fn main() {
```

```
    let float_vector = vec![3.59, -6.25, -0.23, 5.69,
8.42, 1.23];
    let int_vector = vec![0, 10, 20];
    println!("\nfloat_vector printed using while loop:
\n");
    let mut i = 0;
    while i < float_vector.len() {
        println!("{}", float_vector[i]);
        i = i + 1;
    }
    println!("\nint_vector printed using for loop: \n");
    for num in int_vector {
        println!("{}", num);
    }
}
```

Output:

Elements can be added to a vector using the ***push*** method as follows:

<vector variable>.push(<element>);

Example:

num.push(6);

num.push(3);

14. Vectors

Note: A vector must be declared as mutable for the push method to work.

The **vec!** macro is used when a vector needs to be created an initialized. There is another way with which you can create an empty vector and then keep adding elements using the push method. The new method from the **Vec** module is used to create an empty vector as follows:

let mut <vector variable> : Vec<[data type]> = Vec::new();

Example:

let mut phones : Vec<&str> = Vec::new();

Here is a program that shows these concepts in action:

```
fn main() {

    let mut names : Vec<&str> = Vec::new();

    let mut num_vector = vec![1, 0, 3];

    println!("\nnames length: {}\nnum_vector length: {}\n", names.len(), num_vector.len());

    names.push("Igor");
    names.push("Bilal");
    names.push("Silvy");
    names.push("Bob");

    println!("\nnames: {:?}", names);
    println!("\nnum_vector: {:?}", num_vector);
```

```rust
    println!("\nnames length: {}\nnum_vector length: {}\n", names.len(), num_vector.len());
    //Add elements to num_vector
    num_vector.push(2);
    num_vector.push(5);
    println!("\nResults after final updation of vectors:\n");
    println!("\nnames: {:?}", names);
    println!("\nnum_vector: {:?}", num_vector);
    println!("\nnames length: {}\nnum_vector length: {}\n", names.len(), num_vector.len());


}
```

Output:

```
F:\Rust>rustc vector4.rs
F:\Rust>vector4.exe
names length: 0
num_vector length: 3

names: ["Igor", "Bilal", "Silvy", "Bob"]
num_vector: [1, 0, 3]
names length: 4
num_vector length: 3
Results after final updation of vectors:

names: ["Igor", "Bilal", "Silvy", "Bob"]
num_vector: [1, 0, 3, 2, 5]
names length: 4
num_vector length: 5

F:\Rust>
```

15. Strings

A string is a sequence of characters. Rust offers two types of strings – **string literal** and **object type**. A string literal is used when the string is used at compile time. Where as, the object type string is a dynamic heap type string. We have used both types in various programs, let us now revise some of the concepts we already know regrading strings and then learn more.

A **string literal** is of the **&str** data type and can be declared as:

let <string variable>:&str = <Initial value in quotes>;

Example:

let pc_make:&str = "Dell";

Even if the data type &str is not specified, a string defined using the above syntax will be considered as a string literal.

An object type string can be declared using the **String::new()** method. String module is a part of the Rust standard library – **std::String**. The String::new() method creates an empty string. Example:

let <string variable> = String::new();

Example:

let mut msg = String::new();

The functions **push_str** and **push** can be used to append string and character respectively to an object string type. General syntax:

<string variable>.push_str(<string>);

<string variable>.push(<character>);

Example:

msg.push_str("Hello");

msg.push(' ');

msg.push('W');

msg.push('o');

msg.push('r');

msg.push('l');

msg.push('d');

msg.push('!');

Note: The object type string variable should be declared as mutable for **push_str** and **push** functions to work.

Another method of creating an object type string is using the ***String::from*** method:

let <string variable> = String::from(<initial string value>);

Example:

let city = String::from("Kuala Lumpur");

A string literal can be converted to an object type string using the ***to_string()*** function as follows:

let <object type string variable> = <string variable>.to_string();

Example:

15. Strings

let name:&str = "Roger";

let first_name = name.to_string();

let last_name = "Williams".to_string();

The size of a string can be determined using the **len()** function. This function works with both types of strings.

Let us use all these concepts and write a Rust program to create different strings:

```rust
fn main() {
  let name1:&str = "Orin";
  let mut name2 = String::new();
  name2.push_str("Deb");
  let name3 = String::from("Lola");
  let name4 = "Jade".to_string();
  let num:f64 = 54.75;
  let num_str = num.to_string();
    println!("\nname1:   {}   \tLength:   {}", name1, name1.len());
    println!("\nname2:   {}   \tLength:   {}", name2, name2.len());
    println!("\nname3:   {}   \tLength:   {}", name3, name3.len());
```

```
    println!("\nname4:    {}    \tLength:    {}",    name4,
name4.len());
    println!("\nnum_str:  {}   \tLength:    {}\n",   num_str,
num_str.len());
}
```

Output:

```
F:\Rust>rustc string1.rs
F:\Rust>string1.exe
name1: Orin      Length: 4
name2: Deb       Length: 3
name3: Lola      Length: 4
name4: Jade      Length: 4
num_str: 54.75   Length: 5

F:\Rust>_
```

15.1 Concatenation

Two or more object type strings can be joined together using the ***plus (+) operator***. In case a string literal is to be concatenated, it should be converted to object type string first using the ***to_string*** function. Here is the general syntax:

<concatenated string> = <string 1> + &<string 2> + &<string 3> + ... + &<string n>;

Example:

let str5 = str1 + &str2 + &str3 + &str4;

If you want to place a separator between strings such as a white-space or a comma, you can do it as follows:

let str3 = str1 + " " + &str2;

15. Strings

Note: The ampersand (&) symbol prefixed to the string variables is used to fetch the reference to those variables. This is a concept of borrowing and pointers; considered to be quite advanced and is beyond the scope of explanation in this book.

Another way to concatenate strings is by using push and push_str functions to append string values to an object type string. Let us write a program to demonstrate string concatenation:

```rust
fn main() {
    println!("\nConcatenation using + operator:\n");
    let str1 = "This is a".to_string();
    println!("\nstr1: {}", str1);
    let str2 = "string".to_string();
    println!("\nstr2: {}", str2);
    let str3 = "demo".to_string();
    println!("\nstr3: {}", str3);
    let str4 = str1 + " " + &str2 + " " + &str3;
    println!("\nConcatenated string: {}\n", str4);
    println!("\nConcatenation using push_str and push functions:\n");
    let str5:&str = "Another";
    println!("\nstr5: {}", str5);
    let str6:&str = "concatenation";
    println!("\nstr6: {}", str6);
    let str7:&str = "demo";
    println!("\nstr7: {}", str7);
    let mut str8 = String::new();
    str8.push_str(str5);
    str8.push(' ');
    str8.push_str(str6);
    str8.push(' ');
    str8.push_str(str7);
    println!("\nConcatenated string: {}\n", str8);
}
```

Output:

```
F:\Rust>rustc string2.rs
F:\Rust>string2.exe
Concatenation using + operator:
str1: This is a
str2: string
str3: demo
Concatenated string: This is a string demo

Concatenation using push_str and push functions:
str5: Another
str6: concatenation
str7: demo
Concatenated string: Another concatenation demo

F:\Rust>
```

15.2 Replace

A word/pattern can be replaced with a new one using the replace function as follows:

let <new string> = <string variable>.replace(<word/pattern>, <new word/pattern>);

Example:

let s2 = s1.replace("Hi", "Hello");

This function will replace all occurrences of the specified word/pattern with the new one. Here is a program that makes use of the replace function:

```
//String Demo -- Replace
fn main() {
    let str1 = String::from("What they said is, together they can win!");
    println!("\nstr1: {}", str1);
```

```
    let str2 = str1.replace("they", "we");
    println!("\nstr2: {}", str2);
}
```

Output:

```
F:\Rust>rustc string3.rs
F:\Rust>string3.exe
str1: What they said is, together they can win!
str2: What we said is, together we can win!
F:\Rust>
```

15.3 String Tokenization

String tokenization is a process of extracting parts of a string usually marked by a separator character. Rust offers two functions for this purpose – **split_whitespace()** and **split(<separator>)** to tokenize a string by using white-space as separator and a custom character as a separator respectively. Both these function return a collection of sub strings in an iterator. It is best to use these iterators with for loops. Here is a general syntax of these functions:

<string variable>.split_whitespace();

<string variable>.split(<separator>);

Example:

msg1.split_whitespace()

msg2.split(";")

Let us write a program to demonstrate the use of these two functions:

```rust
//String Demo -- Split/Tokenize
fn main() {
    let str1 = String::from("Russia is the largest country by area");
    println!("\nstr1: {}", str1);
    let str2 = String::from("Netherlands,Norway,Japan,USA,India,Singapore");
    println!("\nstr2: {}\n", str2);
    //Tokenize str1 using split_whitespace
    println!("\nTokenized str1 by whitespace:\n");
    for str_token in str1.split_whitespace() {
        println!("{}", str_token);
    }
    println!("\nTokenized str2 by comma:\n");
    //Tokenize str2 using split(",")
    for str_token in str2.split(",") {
        println!("{}", str_token);
    }
}
```

Output:

```
F:\Rust>string4.exe
str1: Russia is the largest country by area
str2: Netherlands,Norway,Japan,USA,India,Singapore

Tokenized str1 by whitespace:

Russia
is
the
largest
country
by
area

Tokenized str2 by comma:

Netherlands
Norway
Japan
USA
India
Singapore

F:\Rust>
```

16. Functions

A function is a piece of code designed to perform a task or a set of tasks. This code can be reused as and when desired thus avoiding the need to write the same code again. For example, we have used the function *read_line* to read user input. Someone has already written code inside this function which interacts with the hardware and facilitates user input. This saves us the trouble of writing our own code to interact with the input hardware and fetch the input. Similarly there are many more functions. In this section, we will learn to write our own functions. When learning functions, this topic can be broadly divided into two categories – function definition and function call. In a function definition you write code for that function, thus defining what that function should do. A function call is where you invoke that function.

16.1 Function Definition

A function can be defined with the *fn* keyword and should be done outside all other functions, including main function. Here is the general syntax of a function that accepts no arguments and returns no value:

fn <function name> () {

　//Function body

}

Example:

fn hello_function () {

println!("\nHello from hello_function!");

}

16.2 Function call

A function can be called from a different function (like main) simply by using the function name. Here is the general syntax to call a function that does not accept any arguments and does not return any value:

<function name>();

Example:

hello_function();

Let us write a program to write a function that accepts no arguments and returns no value. We will call this function from the main function:

```
//Function demo - a function that accepts no
arguments, does not return any values
//Main function
fn main() {
 println!("\nInside main function.\n");
 //Call simple_function
 simple_function();
}
//simple_function definition
fn simple_function() {
 println!("\nInside simple_function.\n");
}
```

16. Functions

Output:

```
F:\Rust>rustc function1.rs
F:\Rust>function1.exe
Inside main function.

Inside simple_function.

F:\Rust>
```

Functions can be placed anywhere in the program as long as they are outside all other functions. Let us take another example where we will have multiple functions and call them from main:

```rust
fn function1() {
 println!("\nInside function1.\n")
}


fn function2() {
 println!("\nInside function2.\n")
}

fn main() {
 println!("\nInside main function.\n");

 function1();

 function2();

 function3();
}

fn function3() {
```

```
println!("\nInside function3.\n")
}
```

Output:

```
F:\Rust>rustc function2.rs
F:\Rust>function2.exe
Inside main function.

Inside function1.

Inside function2.

Inside function3.

F:\Rust>
```

16.3 Functions with parameters/arguments

Parameters or arguments is data sent to a function. This data is received inside variables in the function. A function can be designed to accept parameters/arguments using the following syntax:

fn <function name> (<arg 1: data type 1>, <arg 2: data type 2>, ... <arg n: data type n>) {

//Function body

}

Example:

fn show_data (x: u32, y: u32) {

println!("\n x = {} y = {}", x, y);

}

16. Functions

When calling a function that accepts arguments, the exact number of arguments should be passed in the correct order. General syntax:

<function name>(arg 1, arg 2, ... arg n);

Example:

show_data(1, 2);

Let us write a function which accepts an integer and shows three times its value:

```
fn main() {
   let a:isize = 21;
   println!("\nInside main function.\na = {}", a);
   show_triple(a);
}
fn show_triple(a: isize) {
   println!("\nInside show_triple function.\na = {}, (a x 3) = {}\n", a, (a * 3));
}
```

Output:

```
F:\Rust>rustc function3.rs
F:\Rust>function3.exe
Inside main function.
a = 21
Inside show_triple function.
a = 21, (a x 3) = 63
F:\Rust>
```

125

16.4 Return value

A function can return a value back to the calling function. When a function is designed to return a value, the data type of the value to be returned should be specified. Here is the general syntax:

fn <function name> (<optional arguments>) -> [RETURN TYPE]
{

  //Function body

  return <value/variable/expression>;

}

Example:

fn double_it (x: u32) -> u32 {

  *return (x * 2);*

}

When calling a function that returns a value, a variable should be specified in the calling function to receive the returned value. General syntax:

<variable> = <function name>(<optional arguments>);

Example:

let y = double_it (7);

Let us write a function to accept two integers and return their sum. In the main function, we will set a variable to receive the sum:

16. Functions

```rust
fn add_two_numbers(a: isize, b:isize) -> isize {
    let sum = a + b;
    return sum;
}

fn main() {
    let x:isize = 34;
    let y:isize = 86;
    let s = add_two_numbers(x, y);
    println!("\nx = {} y = {} sum = {}\n", x, y, s);
}
```

Output:

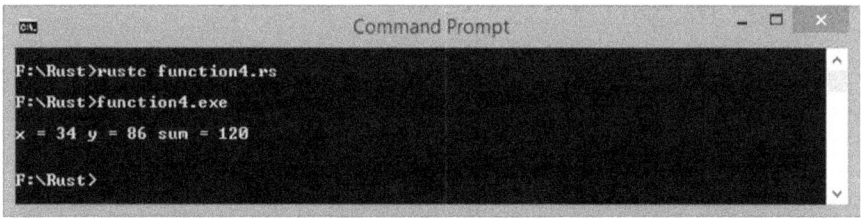

Passing arguments to functions and returning values is an important concept. Let us write another program where we will ask the user to enter two integers, calculate sum, difference, product and quotient using functions:

```rust
fn sum(a: isize, b:isize) -> isize {
    let sum = a + b;
```

```rust
    //Return sum to the calling function
    return sum;
}
fn difference(a: isize, b:isize) -> isize {
    //Subtract b from a, store in d
    let d = a - b;
    //Return d to the calling function
    return d;
}
fn product(a: isize, b:isize) -> isize {
    //Multiply a and b, store in p
    let p = a * b;
    //Return p to the calling function
    return p;
}
fn quotient(a: isize, b:isize) -> f64 {
    //Divide a and b, store in q
    let q:f64 = (a as f64) / (b as f64);
    //Return q to the calling function
    return q;
}
//main function
fn main() {
    //Declare string to store the input in string form
    let mut num1_str = String::new();
    let mut num2_str = String::new();
    println!("\nEnter a number : ");
    //Read the input using stdin, store the string
    //input in num1_str
    std::io::stdin().read_line(&mut num1_str).unwrap();
    //Parse the input and try to convert string
    //equivalent numbers to int
    //Place it into num1
    let num1:isize = num1_str.trim().parse().unwrap();
    println!("\nEnter another number : ");
```

16. Functions

```
    std::io::stdin().read_line(&mut num2_str).unwrap();


    let num2:isize = num2_str.trim().parse().unwrap();

    let s = sum(num1, num2);
    let d = difference(num1, num2);
    let p = product(num1, num2);
    let q = quotient(num1, num2);
    println!("\nSum = {}\nDifference = {} \nProduct = {}\nQuotient = {}\n", s, d, p, q);
}
```

Output:

```
F:\Rust>rustc function6.rs
F:\Rust>function6.exe
Enter a number :
77
Enter another number :
5
Sum = 82
Difference = 72
Product = 385
Quotient = 15.4

F:\Rust>_
```

16.5 Passing arrays and vectors to functions

A function can be defined to accept an array as follows:

fn <function name>(<array variable parameter>:[<type>; <size>]) {

//Function body

}

129

Example:

fn show_array(num_array: [f64; 10]) {

  println!("\n{:?}", num_array);

}

//Function call

show_array(num);

A function can be defined to accept a vector as follows:

fn <function name>(<array variable parameter>:&Vec<[type]>) {

  //Function body

}

Example:

fn show_vector(num_v: &Vec<f64>) {

  println!("\n{:?}", num_v);

}

//Function call

show_vector(num);

Let us write a program to pass an integer array to a function and return the sum of all elements of that array:

```
//Function demo - passing array to a function
fn array_sum(num_arr:[isize;5]) -> isize {
    //Declare and initialize sum
    let mut sum = 0;
    //Loop through array
    for x in num_arr.iter() {
```

16. Functions

```
    sum = sum + x;
  }
  return sum;
}

fn main() {

  let arr = [1, 8, 5, 3, 7];

  let s = array_sum(arr);
  println!("\narr:\n {:?} \n\nSum = {}", arr, s);
}
```

Output:

```
F:\Rust>rustc function5.rs
F:\Rust>function5.exe
arr:
 [1, 8, 5, 3, 7]
Sum = 24
F:\Rust>
```

16.6 Returning a vector from a function

When a function is defined to return a vector, its return type should be set to *Vec<[data type]>*. Let us write a program where we will create two arrays inside main function, pass these to a function where both arrays will be merged into one vector and it will be returned to the main function:

```
fn main() {
  println!("\nInside main function, calling function_1.");

  function_1();
```

```rust
    println!("\nBack inside main function, calling
    function_4.");
    //Call function_4
    function_4();
    println!("\nBack inside main function. Program
    exiting now.\n");
}
fn function_1() {
    println!("\nInside function_1, calling function_2.");
    //Call function_2
    function_2();
}
fn function_2() {
    println!("\nInside function_2, calling function_3.");
    //Call function_3
    function_3();
}
fn function_3() {
    println!("\nInside function_3, returning to the
    calling function.");
}
fn function_4() {
    println!("\nInside function_4, calling function_2.");
    //Call function_2
    function_2();
}
```

Output:

```
F:\Rust>rustc function8.rs
F:\Rust>function8.exe
n1: [20, -95, 74, -23, 67]
n2: [90, -57, 86]
n: [20, -95, 74, -23, 67, 90, -57, 86]

F:\Rust>
```

16.7 Functions calling each other

All functions need not be called from the main function. Any function can call any other function. Here is an example:

```
//Function Demo - functions calling each other
fn main() {
   println!("\nInside main function, calling function_1.");
   //Call function_1
   function_1();
   println!("\nBack inside main function, calling function_4.");
   //Call function_4
   function_4();
   println!("\nBack inside main function. Program exiting now.\n");
}
fn function_1() {
   println!("\nInside function_1, calling function_2.");
   //Call function_2
   function_2();
}
fn function_2() {
   println!("\nInside function_2, calling function_3.");
   //Call function_3
   function_3();
}
fn function_3() {
   println!("\nInside function_3, returning to the calling function.");
}
fn function_4() {
   println!("\nInside function_4, calling function_2.");
   //Call function_2
   function_2();
}
```

Output:

```
F:\Rust>rustc function7.rs
F:\Rust>function7.exe
Inside main function, calling function_1.
Inside function_1, calling function_2.
Inside function_2, calling function_3.
Inside function_3, returning to the calling function.
Back inside main function, calling function_4.
Inside function_4, calling function_2.
Inside function_2, calling function_3.
Inside function_3, returning to the calling function.
Back inside main function. Program exiting now.

F:\Rust>
```

Note:

- A function cannot be defined inside another function and thus has to be present outside all other functions.

- When calling a function that accepts arguments, exact number of arguments should be passed to that function and in the order as specified in the function definition.

- When a function returns a value, its data type should be specified.

- A function can return only one value. However, there are a few workarounds. For example, if more than one value to be returned is of the same data type, those values can be placed inside a vector and the vector can be returned. Another option is to put different values inside a structure and return that structure. This has been covered in the structures chapter.

- A function can call itself. This is known as recursion. However, it is best to not use it.

17. Structures

A structure is a user defined data type which can contain one or more elements of any data type. This is an important tool for dealing with meaningful data such as database records. While we will not go so much in detail but will definitely learn the basic concepts.

A structure can be defined as follows:

struct <name> {

　<field 1>: <data type 1>,

　<field 2>: <data type 2>,

　<field 3>: <data type 3>,

　<field n>: <data type n>

}

Example:

　struct Person {

　name:String,

　age:i32,

　gender:char,

　country:String

　}

When a structure is defined, it is merely a blueprint of what this custom data type should look like. It does not contain any data of its own. An instance of a structure needs to be created and the fields should be initialized. Structure instance is also known as structure variable. The following syntax is used to initialize a structure variable:

let <structure variable> = <structure name> {

<field 1>: <value 1>,

<field 2>: <value 2>,

<field 3>: <value 3>,

<field n>: <value n>

};

Example:

let first_person = Person {

　name: "Yulia",

　age: 41,

　gender: 'F',

　country: "Russia"

};

let second_person = Person {

　name: "Juan",

　age: 62,

　gender: 'M',

　country: "Spain"

};

17. Structures

While structure definition is only an outline of how the custom data type is built internally, a structure variable contains the actual data. For instance, in the above example, the **struct Person** is made up of the fields – *name, age, gender and country*. The structure variables *first_person* and *second_person* have their own copies of *name, age, gender and country*. Fields of a structure variable can be accessed using the dot operator as follows:

<variable> = <struct variable>.field;

Example:

let n = p.name;

let a = p.age;

Let us write a Rust program with a simple structure called Point having the attributes x and y of integer type:

```
struct Point {
  x:i32,
  y:i32
}
fn main() {

  let p1 = Point {
       x: 1,
       y: 2
  };

  let p2 = Point {
       x: 6,
       y: 8
  };
```

```rust
    //Print structure variables
    println!("\nPoint p1:\nx = {}\ty = {}", p1.x, p1.y);
    println!("\nPoint p2:\nx = {}\ty = {}", p2.x, p2.y);
}
```

Output:

```
F:\Rust>rustc structure1.rs
F:\Rust>structure1.exe
Point p1:
x = 1    y = 2
Point p2:
x = 6    y = 8
F:\Rust>
```

Let us consider another program with struct Person stated as an example earlier in this chapter:

```rust
//Structure demo 2
//Declare a structure
struct Person {
  name:String,
  age:i32,
  gender:char,
  country:String
}
fn main() {
    //Initialize a structure variable
    let p1 = Person {
        name: String::from("Fiona"),
        age: 29,
        gender: 'F',
        country: String::from("Brazil")
    };
    let p2 = Person {
        name: String::from("Stuart"),
        age: 33,
        gender: 'M',
```

17. Structures

```
        country: String::from("UK")
    };
    let p3 = Person {
        name: String::from("Lily"),
        age: 27,
        gender: 'F',
        country: String::from("Ireland")
    };

    println!("\nPerson p1\nname: {}\nage: {}\ngender: {}\ncountry: {}\n",   p1.name,   p1.age,   p1.gender, p1.country);
    println!("\nPerson p2\nname: {}\nage: {}\ngender: {}\ncountry: {}\n",   p2.name,   p2.age,   p2.gender, p2.country);
    println!("\nPerson p3\nname: {}\nage: {}\ngender: {}\ncountry: {}\n",   p3.name,   p3.age,   p3.gender, p3.country);
}
```

Output:

```
F:\Rust>rustc structure2.rs
F:\Rust>structure2.exe
Person p1
name: Fiona
age: 29
gender: F
country: Brazil

Person p2
name: Stuart
age: 33
gender: M
country: UK

Person p3
name: Lily
age: 27
gender: F
country: Ireland

F:\Rust>
```

A structure variable can be passed to a function as an argument. In the function definition, the data type of the receiving argument should be specified as the structure name. For example, if you plan to pass a structure variable of struct Person type, your function definition could look like this:

fn function1 (p: Person) {

// Statements

}

Following is a program which demonstrates this concept:

```
//Structure demo 3 -- Passing structure variable to a function
//Declare a structure
struct Country {
  name:String,
  capital:String,
  continent:String,
  calling_code:i32
}
fn show_country(c: Country){
  println!("\nCountry Name: {}", c.name);
  println!("Capital: {}", c.capital);
  println!("Continent: {}", c.continent);
  println!("Dialing Code: +{}\n", c.calling_code);
}
fn main() {
  //Initialize a structure variables
  let c1 = Country {
      name: String::from("Australia"),
      capital: String::from("Canberra"),
      continent: String::from("Australia"),
      calling_code: 61
```

17. Structures

```
    };
    let c2 = Country {
        name: String::from("UK"),
        capital: String::from("London"),
        continent: String::from("Europe"),
        calling_code: 44
    };
    let c3 = Country {
        name: String::from("South Africa"),
        capital: String::from("Cape Town"),
        continent: String::from("Africa"),
        calling_code: 27
    };
    let c4 = Country {
        name: String::from("Japan"),
        capital: String::from("Tokyo"),
        continent: String::from("Asia"),
        calling_code: 81
    };
    let c5 = Country {
        name: String::from("Canada"),
        capital: String::from("Ottawa"),
        continent: String::from("North America"),
        calling_code: 1
    };

    show_country(c1);
    show_country(c2);
    show_country(c3);
    show_country(c4);
    show_country(c5);
}
```

Output:

```
F:\Rust>rustc structure3.rs

F:\Rust>structure3.exe
Country Name: Australia
Capital: Canberra
Continent: Australia
Dialing Code: +61

Country Name: UK
Capital: London
Continent: Europe
Dialing Code: +44

Country Name: South Africa
Capital: Cape Town
Continent: Africa
Dialing Code: +27

Country Name: Japan
Capital: Tokyo
Continent: Asia
Dialing Code: +81

Country Name: Canada
Capital: Ottawa
Continent: North America
Dialing Code: +1
```

Just like a function can accept structure variables as arguments, a structure variable can also be returned by a function. If you want to return a structure variable of **Person** type, you need to set the return type of the function to **Person**. Your function definition may look like:

fn function1 () -> Person{

　//Statements

　//Mandatory return statement

}

Here is a program that shows how it works:

```
//Structure demo 4 -- returning a struct variable
//Declare a structure
struct Data {
```

17. Structures

```rust
    name:String,
    age:i32,
    gender:char,
    city:String,
    country:String
}
fn get_data() -> Data {

    let d1 = Data {
        name: String::from("Antonio"),
        age: 33,
        gender: 'M',
        city: String::from("Milan"),
        country: String::from("Italy")
    };
    return d1;
}
fn show_data(p: Data) {
    println!("\nname: {}\nage: {}\ngender: {}\ncity: {}\ncountry: {}\n", p.name, p.age, p.gender, p.city, p.country);
}
fn main() {

    let d = get_data();

    show_data(d);
}
```

Output:

```
F:\Rust>rustc structure4.rs
F:\Rust>structure4.exe
name: Antonio
age: 33
gender: M
city: Milan
country: Italy
```

18. Command Line Arguments

Command line arguments are inputs given to an application via the command line interface at the time of running the application. When an application is designed to accept command line arguments, the compilation procedure remains the same while the execution procedure involves an additional step. Let us assume that we have a program called xyz.rs which is designed to accept command line arguments. We will compile it as:

rustc xyz.rs

If the compilation is successful, an executable binary will be generated (xyz.exe on Windows and xyz on Linux/MAC). Command line arguments will have to be passed while executing this binary as follows:

On Windows:

<application name>.exe <arg 1> <arg 2> <arg 3> ... <arg n>

Example:

xyz.exe 1 hello 6

On Linux/MAC:

<application name> <arg 1> <arg 2> <arg 3> ... <arg n>

Example:

xyz 8 d 1 A 3

A white-space is used to mark one argument. Hence, when there are multiple arguments to be passed, they have to be separated by a space. An application receives arguments in string format only. Even if you pass numbers, they will be read as strings. If you want a string with spaces in it to be treated as one command line argument, it needs to be enclosed within double quotes.

18.1 Fetching command line arguments

There are various functions inside the **env** module of the Rust standard library (**std**) that are used when dealing with command line arguments. We will be making use of this module and hence the following statement will be present in all programs which need the env module:

use std::env;

A function called **collect()** is used to fetch all the command line arguments. This function returns a vector with all the arguments that are passed. The first element of this vector, i.e. at index 0 is the name of the program. Even if you do not pass any arguments, the name of the application will be fetched and placed at index 0 of this vector.

Here is the general syntax of using the collect function:

let <arguments vector>: Vec<String> = env::args().collect();

Example:

let args: Vec<String> = env::args().collect();

Let us write a Rust program to fetch the arguments, print the vector and its size:

18. Command Line Arguments

```
use std::env;
fn main() {
    let args: Vec<String> = env::args().collect();
    println!("Command line arguments: \n{:?}\nTotal number of arguments: {}\nArguments passed: {}", args, args.len(), (args.len() - 1));
}
```

Output:

```
F:\Rust>rustc args1.rs

F:\Rust>args1.exe
Command line arguments:
["args1.exe"]
Total number of arguments: 1
Arguments passed: 0

F:\Rust>args1.exe 45 dollar 9.5
Command line arguments:
["args1.exe", "45", "dollar", "9.5"]
Total number of arguments: 4
Arguments passed: 3

F:\Rust>args1.exe "Hello World !!!" 100 500 "Rust eBook"
Command line arguments:
["args1.exe", "Hello World !!!", "100", "500", "Rust eBook"]
Total number of arguments: 5
Arguments passed: 4

F:\Rust>
```

18.2 Numbers as command line arguments

Since all command line arguments are read as strings, when we pass numbers, we will have to parse that particular argument to convert it to an appropriate type. We have done this several times especially when working with user input. *Section 10.1* contains details about parsing a number in string form to a numeric data type. Let us write a program to read two floating point numbers as command line arguments and calculate their sum, difference, product and quotient:

```rust
//Command line arguments demo 2
//Use env module from the Rust standard library std
use std::env;
fn sum(a: f64, b:f64) -> f64 {
    //Add a and b, store in sum
    let sum = a + b;
    //Return sum to the calling function
    return sum;
}
fn difference(a: f64, b:f64) -> f64 {
    //Subtract b from a, store in d
    let d = a - b;
    //Return d to the calling function
    return d;
}
fn product(a: f64, b:f64) -> f64 {
    //Multiply a and b, store in p
    let p = a * b;
    //Return p to the calling function
    return p;
}
fn quotient(a: f64, b:f64) -> f64 {
    //Divide a and b, store in q
    let q:f64 = a / b;
    //Return q to the calling function
    return q;
}
fn main() {
    //Call collect() function to fetch all the arguments
    let args: Vec<String> = env::args().collect();
    //Make sure that the user passes 2 arguments
    if args.len() != 3 {
```

18. Command Line Arguments

```
        println!("\nPlease pass exactly two numbers as arguments.")
    }
    else {
        //Parse args[1] and args[2] as f64
        let num1:f64 = args[1].trim().parse().unwrap();
        let num2:f64 = args[2].trim().parse().unwrap();
        let s = sum(num1, num2);
        let d = difference(num1, num2);
        let p = product(num1, num2);
        let q = quotient(num1, num2);
        println!("\nSum = {}\nDifference = {} \nProduct = {}\nQuotient = {}\n", s, d, p, q);
    }
}
```

Output:

```
F:\Rust>rustc args2.rs
F:\Rust>args2.exe 162.7235 59.0812
Sum = 221.8047
Difference = 103.6423
Product = 9613.8996482
Quotient = 2.7542348496645292

F:\Rust>
```

19. Programming Examples

We have learnt many different concepts throughout the course of this book. Let us take up a few programming examples to revise and strengthen those concepts further.

19.1 Fibonacci Series

Fibonacci series begins with the terms 0 and 1. The next term is derived by adding the previous two terms. The series looks like this – 0, 1, 1, 2, 3, 5, 8, 13, 21, 34, 55, 89, ... Here is the program:

```
//Fibonacci series
fn main() {
   let mut previous = 0;
   let mut current = 1;
   let mut next:isize;
   let mut count = 0;
   //To start with, variable to store the input in
   string form
   let mut num_str = String::new();
   println!("\nEnter the number of terms :");
   //Read the input from stdin, store the string
   input in num_str
   std::io::stdin().read_line(&mut num_str).unwrap();
   //Convert the input from string to isize and
   assign it to num
   let num: isize = num_str.trim().parse().unwrap();
   if num < 2 {
       println!("\nFibonacci series contains a minimum of two terms.\n");
   }
   else {
       print!("\n{} {} ", previous, current);
       while count < (num - 2) {
```

```
            next = previous + current;
            previous = current;
            current = next;
            print!("{} ", next);
            count = count + 1;
        }
    }
    println!("\n");
}
```

Output:

```
F:\Rust>rustc fibo.rs
F:\Rust>fibo.exe
Enter the number of terms :
20
0 1 1 2 3 5 8 13 21 34 55 89 144 233 377 610 987 1597 2584 4181

F:\Rust>_
```

19.2 Sum of digits of an integer

Let us write a program to read an integer from the user and compute the sum of all the digits of an integer:

```
//Sum of digits
fn main() {
    let mut sum: isize = 0;
    //Declare mutable strings to store the input in string form
    let mut num_str = String::new();
    println!("\nEnter a number :");
    //Read the input using stdin, store the string input in num_str
    std::io::stdin().read_line(&mut num_str).unwrap();
    //Parse the input and try to convert string equivalent numbers to int
```

19. Programming Examples

```
    let         mut        num:         isize        =
num_str.trim().parse().unwrap();
    while num > 0 {
        sum = sum + (num % 10);
        num = num / 10;
    }
    println!("Sum = {}\n", sum);
}
```

Output:

```
F:\Rust>rustc sumdigits.rs
F:\Rust>sumdigits.exe
Enter a number :
52413
Sum = 15

F:\Rust>
```

19.3 Reverse a number

Let us write a program to read an integer from the user and reverse it:

```
fn main() {
  let mut rev: isize = 0;

  let mut num_str = String::new();
  println!("\nEnter a number :");

  std::io::stdin().read_line(&mut num_str).unwrap();

    let mut num: isize =
num_str.trim().parse().unwrap();
```

```
while num > 0 {
    rev = (rev * 10) + (num % 10);
    num = num / 10;
}
println!("Reverse = {}\n", rev);
}
```

Output:

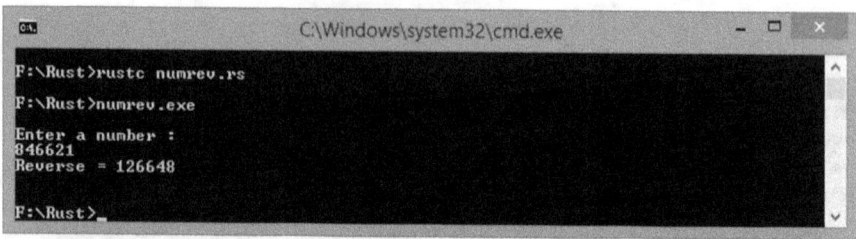

19.4 Greatest number from command line arguments

We will write a program to accept numbers as command line arguments and determine the greatest number:

```
//Greatest from the command line arguments
use std::env;
fn main() {
  let mut count = 1;
  let mut greatest: isize;
  //Call collect() function to fetch all the
arguments
  let args: Vec<String> = env::args().collect();
  //Make sure that the user passes 2 arguments
  if args.len() < 3 {
      println!("\nPlease pass at least two numbers as command line arguments.")
  }
  else {
      let first:isize =
args[1].trim().parse().unwrap();
```

19. Programming Examples

```
        greatest = first;
        while count < (args.len() - 1) {
            let                num:isize =
args[count].trim().parse().unwrap();
            if num > greatest {
                greatest = num;
            }
            count = count + 1;
        }
        println!("\nGreatest: {}\n", greatest);
    }
}
```

Output:

```
F:\Rust>rustc cmdgreatest.rs
F:\Rust>cmdgreatest.exe 45 98 -34 12 -71 22
Greatest: 98

F:\Rust>
```

19.5 Bubble Sort Algorithm

Let us write a program to sort an array using the bubble sort algorithm:

```
fn main() {

    let mut num_str = String::new();

    let mut i: usize = 0;
    let mut j: usize;

    let mut temp: isize;
```

```
    //Declare a mutable array of 5 integers, fill with
zeros
    let mut num_array: [isize;5] = [0;5];
    //Loop from 0 to 4, five times
    while i < 5 {
        //Prompt the user to enter a number
        println!("\nEnter a number at index {}: ", i);
        //Clear num_str so that previous input is
flushed
        num_str.clear();
        //Read the input using stdin, store the string
input in num_str
        std::io::stdin().read_line(&mut
num_str).unwrap();
        //Parse the input and try to convert string
equivalent numbers to int
        //Place it into an array
        num_array[i] = num_str.trim().parse().unwrap();
        //Increment i
        i += 1;
    }
    println!("\nOriginal array: {:?} ", num_array);
    //Bubble Sort
    i = 0;
    while i < num_array.len() {
        j = 0;
        while j < (num_array.len() - i - 1) {
            if num_array[j] > num_array[j + 1] {
                temp = num_array[j];
                num_array[j] = num_array[j + 1];
                num_array[j + 1] = temp;
            }
            j = j + 1;
        }
        i = i + 1;
    }
    println!("\nSorted array: {:?} ", num_array);
}
```

Output:

```
F:\Rust>rustc bubblesort.rs
F:\Rust>bubblesort.exe
Enter a number at index 0:
42
Enter a number at index 1:
94
Enter a number at index 2:
0
Enter a number at index 3:
82
Enter a number at index 4:
35
Original array: [42, 94, 0, 82, 35]
Sorted array: [0, 35, 42, 82, 94]
F:\Rust>
```

19.6 Array Reversal

In this program, we will read an array of 5 integers and reverse it:

```
fn main(){

    let mut num_str = String::new();

    let mut i = 0;

    let mut temp :isize;

    let mut num_array: [isize;5] = [0;5];

    while i < 5 {

        println!("\nEnter a number at index {}: ", i);
```

```
        //Clear num_str so that previous input is
flushed
        num_str.clear();
        //Read the input using stdin, store the string
input in num_str
        std::io::stdin().read_line(&mut
num_str).unwrap();
        //Parse the input and try to convert string
equivalent numbers to int
        //Place it into an array
        num_array[i] = num_str.trim().parse().unwrap();
        //Increment i
        i += 1;
    }
    println!("\nOriginal array: {:?} ", num_array);
    i = 0;
    while i < num_array.len()/2 {
        temp = num_array[i];
        num_array[i] = num_array[num_array.len() - 1 -
i];
        num_array[num_array.len() - 1 - i] = temp;
        i += 1;
    }
    println!("\nReversed array: {:?} ", num_array);
}
```

19. Programming Examples

Output:

```
F:\Rust>rustc arrayrev.rs
F:\Rust>arrayrev.exe
Enter a number at index 0:
6
Enter a number at index 1:
-3
Enter a number at index 2:
8
Enter a number at index 3:
1
Enter a number at index 4:
5
Original array: [6, -3, 8, 1, 5]
Reversed array: [5, 1, 8, -3, 6]
F:\Rust>
```

19.7 Least Common Multiple (LCM)

Here is a Rust program that finds the least common multiple of two numbers:

```rust
fn main() {

    let mut num1_str = String::new();
    let mut num2_str = String::new();

    println!("\nEnter a number :");

    std::io::stdin().read_line(&mut num1_str).unwrap();

    println!("\nEnter another number :");

    std::io::stdin().read_line(&mut num2_str).unwrap();
```

```rust
//Parse the input and try to convert string
equivalent numbers to int
    let num1: isize = num1_str.trim().parse().unwrap();
    let num2: isize = num2_str.trim().parse().unwrap();
    let mut max: isize;
    if num1 >= num2 {
        max = num1;
    }
    else {
        max = num2;
    }
    loop {
    if (max % num1 == 0) && (max % num2 == 0) {
            println!("\nLCM of {} and {} is {}\n", num1, num2, max);
            break;
    }
        max = max + 1;
    }
}
```

Output:

```
F:\Rust>rustc lcm.rs
F:\Rust>lcm
Enter a number :
4
Enter another number :
6
LCM of 4 and 6 is 12

F:\Rust>
```

19.8 Greatest Common Divisor (GCD)

Here is a Rust program that finds the least common multiple of two numbers:

19. Programming Examples

```rust
fn main() {
    let mut num1_str = String::new();
    let mut num2_str = String::new();
    println!("\nEnter a number :");
    std::io::stdin().read_line(&mut num1_str).unwrap();
    println!("\nEnter another number :");
    std::io::stdin().read_line(&mut num2_str).unwrap();
    let num1: isize = num1_str.trim().parse().unwrap();
    let num2: isize = num2_str.trim().parse().unwrap();
    let mut numerator: isize;
    let mut denominator: isize;
    let mut remainder: isize;
    let gcd: isize;
    if num1 > num2 {
    numerator = num1;
    denominator = num2;
    }
    else {
    numerator = num2;
    denominator = num1;
    }
    remainder = numerator % denominator;
    while remainder != 0 {
    numerator = denominator;
    denominator = remainder;
```

```
        remainder = numerator % denominator;
    }
    gcd = denominator;
    println!("\nGCD of {} and {} is {}\n", num1, num2, gcd);
}
```

Output:

```
F:\Rust>rustc gcd.rs
F:\Rust>gcd
Enter a number :
88
Enter another number :
33
GCD of 88 and 33 is 11

F:\Rust>
```

19.9 Prime or Composite

Let us write a program to check whether the given number is prime or composite:

```
//Prime Composite
fn main() {
    //Declare mutable strings to store the input in string form
    let mut num_str = String::new();
    println!("\nEnter a number :");
    //Read the input using stdin, store the string input in num_str
    std::io::stdin().read_line(&mut num_str).unwrap();
    //Parse the input and try to convert string equivalent numbers to int
    let num: isize = num_str.trim().parse().unwrap();
    let mut i = 2;
    let mut flag: bool = false;
```

19. Programming Examples

```rust
    while i < num {
        if num % i == 0 {
            flag = true;
            break;
        }
        i += 1;
    }
    if flag {
        println!("\n{} is composite.\n", num);
    }
    else {
        println!("\n{} is prime.\n", num);
    }
}
```

Output:

```
F:\Rust>rustc primeornot.rs
F:\Rust>primeornot.exe
Enter a number :
2

2 is prime.

F:\Rust>primeornot.exe
Enter a number :
6

6 is composite.

F:\Rust>primeornot.exe
Enter a number :
23

23 is prime.

F:\Rust>
```

20. Final Words

Programming languages such as C/C++ are here to stay. They are not going anywhere at least for the next few years or even decades because of many reasons. One of them is that programs written in these languages can be compiled to a native code for a particular platform using the appropriate compiler. As time went by, people started looking for alternatives to C/C++ to target native platforms. This is where Rust comes in. It is just not ready to replace C/C++ and may never will but there is no doubt that it is a viable alternative. The Linux Kernel is entirely written in C and assembly language wherever necessary. Now, it is possible to write individual kernel modules using Rust. A microkernel based Unix-like operating system called Redox has been written using Rust and assembly language.

Rust is not just meant for system programming, you can do a lot of other things with it such as build libraries, desktop apps, embedded applications, web services, etc.

Whether you are a beginner programmer or already know a few programming languages, there is a good chance that you will come across Rust related projects in the future if you keep looking at the right places.

I have tried my best to explain the basic concepts of Rust in this book. If you would like to learn more, there is plenty of Rust learning material out there on the internet. A few searches on the search engines will bring several results. This book was written during the COVID-19 pandemic during which the IT industry started undergoing several changes. One of them was increased support for the work-from-home model. If you are looking to build a career in software development, knowledge of Rust will definitely give you an edge and with the work-from-home culture, you may even be able to build a career sitting at home.

Wishing you all the very best! Hope you have learned something of value through this book!

If you enjoyed this book as much as I've enjoyed writing it, you can subscribe* to my email list for exclusive content and sneak peaks of my future books.

Visit the link below:

http://eepurl.com/du_L4n

OR

Use the QR Code:

(*Must be 13 years or older to subscribe)

www.ingramcontent.com/pod-product-compliance
Lightning Source LLC
Chambersburg PA
CBHW072029230526
45466CB00020B/1138